Homeland Security Assessment Manual

Also Available from ASQ Quality Press:

Insights to Performance Excellence 2004: An Inside Look at the 2004 Baldrige Award Criteria
Mark L. Blazey

From Baldrige to the Bottom Line: A Road Map for Organizational Change and Improvement
David W. Hutton

Quality into the 21st Century: Perspectives on Quality and Competitiveness for Sustained Performance
International Academy for Quality

Principles and Practices of Organizational Performance Excellence
Thomas J. Cartin

Quality's Greatest Hits: Classic Wisdom from the Leaders of Quality
Zigmund Bluvband

Certified Quality Manager Handbook, Second Edition
Duke Okes and Russell T. Westcott, editors

From Quality to Business Excellence: A Systems Approach to Management
Charles G. Cobb

The Executive Guide to Improvement and Change
G. Dennis Beecroft, Grace L. Duffy, John W. Moran

Customer Centered Six Sigma: Linking Customers, Process improvement, and Financial Results
Earl Naumann and Steven H. Hoisington

To request a complimentary catalog of ASQ Quality Press publications, call 800-248-1946, or visit our Web site at http://qualitypress.asq.org.

Homeland Security Assessment Manual

A Comprehensive Organizational Assessment Based on Baldrige Criteria

Donald C. Fisher, Ph.D.

ASQ Quality Press
Milwaukee, Wisconsin

American Society for Quality, Quality Press, Milwaukee 53203

© 2005 by American Society for Quality

All rights reserved. Published 2004

Printed in the United States of America

12 11 10 09 08 07 06 05 04   5 4 3 2 1

Library of Congress Cataloging-in-Publication Data

Fisher, Donald C.

  Homeland security assessment manual : a comprehensive organizational assessment
    based on Baldrige criteria / Donald C. Fisher.

      p. cm.

  Includes bibliographical references and index.

  ISBN 0-87389-640-8 (alk. paper)

  1. Emergency management—United States—Handbooks, manuals, etc.   2. Civil defense—
  United States—Handbooks, manuals, etc.   3. National security—United States—
  Handbooks, manuals, etc.   4. Terrorism—Prevention—Government policy—United
  States—Handbooks, manuals, etc.   I. Title.

  HV551.3.F57 2005

  658.4'73—dc22   2004016879

ISBN 0-87389-640-8

Publisher: William A. Tony

Acquisitions Editor: Annemieke Hytinen

Project Editor: Paul O'Mara

Production Administrator: Randall Benson

Special Marketing Representative: David Luth

ASQ Mission: The American Society for Quality advances individual, organizational, and community excellence worldwide through learning, quality improvement, and knowledge exchange.

Attention Bookstores, Wholesalers, Schools, and Corporations: ASQ Quality Press books, videotapes, audiotapes, and software are available at quantity discounts with bulk purchases for business, educational, or instructional use. For information, please contact ASQ Quality Press at 800-248-1946, or write to ASQ Quality Press, P.O. Box 3005, Milwaukee, WI 53201-3005.

To place orders or to request a free copy of the ASQ Quality Press Publications Catalog, including ASQ membership information, call 800-248-1946. Visit our Web site at www.asq.org or http://qualitypress.asq.org.

Quality Press
600 N. Plankinton Avenue
Milwaukee, Wisconsin 53203
Call toll free 800-248-1946
Fax 414-272-1734
www.asq.org
http://qualitypress.asq.org
http://standardsgroup.asq.org
E-mail: authors@asq.org

∞ Printed on acid-free paper

This book is dedicated to the memories of my father, Alvin G. Fisher,
a World War II veteran, watchmaker, and jeweler, and my father-in-law, Ernest M. Madrey,
a farmer, carpenter, and youth advisor to
4-H programs for over 30 years. Both men were exemplary in
providing homeland security to their families and communities
over their entire lifetimes.

Contents

CD-ROM Contents

Organizational Overview
Category 1: Leadership
Category 2: Strategic Planning
Category 3: Customer and Market Focus
Category 4: Measurement, Analysis, and Knowledge Management
Category 5: Human Resource Focus
Category 6: Process Management
Category 7: Business Results
Summary of Assessment Items for Homeland Security (Score sheet)
Hierarchy of Homeland Assessment Needs
Transformation of Assessment Findings
Strategic Planning Worksheet
Quick and Easy Supplier/Customer Assessment for Homeland Security
(Based on Baldrige Criteria)
Homeland Security Benchmarking Process
Homeland Security Documentation List
Homeland Security Plan and Budget

Foreword

For the first time in America's history, the private sector is on the front lines of the battlefield in global terrorism—a target, perhaps even a pathway, for attack on our economic infrastructure. Increasingly terrorists seek mass disruption, along with mass destruction. The nation's critical infrastructure, facilities and companies are at risk—and vulnerable.

Although federal and state governments have the principal responsibility to protect American citizens from attack, they face one central dilemma: Critical infrastructures and economic assets are largely privately owned. As a result, public safety increasingly depends on private sector initiatives.

The Council on Competitiveness, a nonprofit, bipartisan organization whose members are chief executive officers, university presidents, and labor leaders, believes that a new private sector paradigm for security is needed. Traditionally, security has been a matter of guards, gates, and guns, seen as a sunk cost for business that drains profits from the bottom line. But new management vision, technologies, risk management tools, and workforce training opportunities offer the potential to achieve higher security and positive economic benefits: new market opportunities, productivity gains, customer confidence, and competitive advantage.

For example, information technology–based identification, tracking, and verification systems in container cargo, for example, should not only increase security of shipments, but also enable just-in-time logistics. Mobile intruder detection technologies could serve a dual purpose of security and inventory management. Sophisticated electronic access control systems that also provide time and attendance and payroll data will reduce security labor costs, increase security effectiveness, and provide a more accurate and efficient method of managing a workforce. Improvements in security against agroterrorism have the potential to halt the growing threat of naturally occurring foodborne and animal-related illnesses as well.

This book makes clear that there is no intrinsic reason why security need be fundamentally different from quality or safety, which have demonstrated economic returns. It is instructive to remember that, in the 1980s, quality was viewed as an expensive luxury rather than a core business process with the potential to reduce cycle time and costs. After the disaster in Bhopal, leaders in the chemical industry demonstrated that improved safety precautions could increase efficiency and drive costs down.

Government cannot lead this effort; it must be driven by the private sector. Although a well-placed terrorist attack has the potential to cripple the country economically, any attempt by government to impose a security regime on the private sector, ironically, could have exactly the same result. Only the private sector is able to design an integrated security approach that protects productivity and competitiveness. This book creates a framework for organizations to begin the critical process of reassessing (and discarding) old views about security in favor of integrating security into their business model.

Creating the right balance between competitiveness and security is the critical challenge. There can be no security without economic vitality, just as there can be no economic vitality without a secure environment in which to live and work.

Debra Van Opstal
Senior vice president, policy and programs
Council on Competitiveness
Washington, D.C.

Preface

This manual has been written as a result of the author's involvement in conducting more than 100 organizational assessments based on the Malcolm Baldrige Criteria for Performance Excellence since 1992. Many organizations have embraced the concept of improving overall performance by using the Baldrige Criteria as a benchmark to gauge their strengths and opportunities for improvement and as a measurement of their overall alignment and integration of key processes.

Since the shocking attack on our country on September 11, 2001, our nation has made great strides in improving homeland security. Individual citizens, industry, and government leaders from all spectrums of American society have become involved in this national obsession to ensure our national security. Many steps have been taken to ensure that our nation is secure from terrorist attempts to unravel our nation as a whole and the public and private institutions and organizations that support this nation's infrastructure.

Terrorists are strategic in selecting targets based on organizational weaknesses and vulnerabilities within our nation's infrastructure. Our nation consists of an infinite array of potential targets that can be attacked through a variety of methods. Actions such as inducement of computer viruses, destruction of computer operating systems, exposure of citizens to biological and chemical agents, massive disruption of high-profile events, manipulation of financial systems, mass-casualty incidents, and interference with major transportation systems are only a few of the horrific activities that terrorists might use to cause major upsets within our society.

The Department of Homeland Security has been established to ensure greater accountability for the nation's critical homeland security mission and to provide a unified approach among agencies responsible for safeguarding the nation. However, at the present time no consistent holistic approach has been defined for public and private organizations. Public and private organizations do not currently have a consistent process to assess their own overall homeland security readiness and vulnerability in the event of a major terrorist attack upon their organizational infrastructure. This author has developed a manual that an organization can use to conduct an internal self-assessment to gauge its overall readiness and vulnerability regarding homeland security. This homeland security manual based on Baldrige Criteria is written as an assessment tool for public and private organizations to measure their overall vulnerability to corporate sabotage and terrorist attacks.

Using the Baldrige Criteria to help address overall homeland security issues within an organization aligns the highly respected Baldrige national criteria for performance excellence with very critical homeland security issues. Public and private organizations must address these issues to ensure a safe work environment for both their employees and those who use their products and services. The Council on Competitiveness in Washington, D.C., has established a homeland security model for private organizations. The Council on Competitiveness noted that the "balance between competitiveness and security is a critical national challenge" (see Appendix C).

The first line of defense for homeland security is this nation's public and private organizations. These organizations comprise the infrastructure that supports our nation's security. This nation cannot be safe until organizations assess their overall homeland security vulnerability and develop a comprehensive homeland security plan based on their assessment findings.

This comprehensive manual will aid an organization's quest to create and maintain a safe work environment for its employees, suppliers, partners, and customers. The stability of this nation rests on the strength and trust of our public and private organizations.

Introduction

The terrorist threat to America's infrastructure takes many forms, has many places to hide, and is often invisible. The need for homeland security is not tied to any specific threat. The need for homeland security is tied to the underlying vulnerability of American infrastructure in general, and specifically to various public and private organizations that comprise that infrastructure.

The unprecedented national response to homeland security began literally minutes after the first plane struck the World Trade Center in New York City on September 11, 2001. Since September 11, the highest levels within U.S. government and their various agencies have gone to enormous lengths to identify the most vulnerable potential targets and critical infrastructure in the United States. Potential targets identified include airports, sea and water ports, nuclear facilities, dams, water and sewer plants, electric power plants, gas pipelines, dams and bridges, and biological and chemical facilities. In addition, high profile events, holidays, and landmarks, such as the Olympics, Super Bowl, New Year's Eve celebration at Times Square in New York City, Christmas, July 4, and numerous other national events and historical landmarks that involve thousands of American citizens and public and private organizations, remain ongoing targets for terrorists.

The National Governor's Association has estimated that states have spent at least $650 million to protect their infrastructure since September 11, 2001.[1]

The United States had never had a national strategy for homeland security until President George W. Bush issued Executive Order 13228, Section 2, on October 8, 2001, establishing the Office of Homeland Security and former Pennsylvania Governor Tom Ridge as director. On January 24, 2003, Ridge became the first Secretary of the Department of Homeland Security. The national strategy took more than eight months to complete and involved thousands of public and private stakeholders.

This manual, with its incorporation of Baldrige criteria, will aid an organization's self-assessment process by keeping it simple and involving a number of various levels of employees in the process. The manual is designed to encourage participation throughout the organization's workforce through assessment teams who ask questions and from those who answer questions regarding homeland security. Total workforce involvement can include up to 200 employees. This assessment process helps an organization determine how holistically integrated the organization is in securing a safe work environment for its employees, suppliers, partners, and customers regarding homeland security.

Homeland Security Resources

Presently, there exist several resources for homeland security planning for cities and towns. The Kentucky League of Cities and the NewCities Foundation have developed an exemplary four-step process for hometown security planning. The process promotes cities and towns:

- Establishing a planning team
- Analyzing capabilities and hazards

- Developing the plan
- Implementing the plan[2]

Other state agencies have provided similar information for elected officials within their states. An example presented to local governments as a practical tool for first steps in homeland security preparation by the National League of Cities includes:

First Steps for Preparedness

- Systematically evaluate current capabilities and deficiencies.
- Perform a risk assessment and vulnerability analysis of the community.
- Ensure that local hospitals are prepared to treat victims of a terrorist attack.
- Meet with those responsible for emergency medical services to assess their current scope of practice as it pertains to terrorist events.
- Provide frequent, brief training programs to medical personnel to ensure their participation in the preparedness process.
- Evaluate the current capabilities of the fire department's response to HAZMAT incidents.
- Cross-train the appropriate responders to avoid having to create and fund additional response teams.
- Develop mutual aid agreements with surrounding communities to ensure better use of existing resources during any type of disaster.
- Incorporate the business community into the planning process.[3]

Homeland security is presently being addressed extensively throughout the nation among state and local levels of government. They have the responsibility for funding, preparing, and operating emergency services that will respond in the event of a terrorist attack.

Public and private sector organizations, the nation's principal provider of goods and services, provide 85 percent of the nation's infrastructure, according to the "National Strategy for Homeland Security Report" issued during July 2002. Public and private sector organizations are key homeland security partners to state and local governments and deliver information systems, ship packages, provide transportation, produce vaccines, manufacture detection devices, and supply utilities and other critical services and technologies and innovations that help secure the homeland.[4]

National Strategy for Homeland Security

The national strategy for homeland security aligns homeland security functions into six critical mission areas: (1) intelligence and warning, (2) border and transportation security, (3) domestic counterterrorism, (4) protecting critical infrastructure, (5) defending against catastrophic terrorism, and (6) emergency preparedness and response. The first three critical mission areas focus on prevention of terrorist attacks, the next two on reducing vulnerabilities, and the final one on a minimization of damage and recovery from the attack.[5]

Protecting America's public/private sector organizational infrastructure presents a formidable challenge. This nation's critical public/private sector infrastructure changes as rapidly as the marketplace. Not all terrorist attacks can be prevented, but they can be significantly reduced by public/private sector organizations who conduct holistic assessments of their infrastructure and work in partnership with federal, state, and local homeland security initiatives.

This manual has been developed for public and private sector organizations to use as a template to assess their overall internal homeland security readiness and vulnerability in the case of a major security threat to their organizational infrastructure.

Baldrige Criteria for Performance Excellence

Many public and private organizations have been using the Malcolm Baldrige Criteria for Performance Excellence since its founding in 1987 for internal self-assessment to measure their organization's performance excellence against this national quality standard of performance criteria.

The Malcolm Baldrige National Quality Improvement Act of 1987 was signed by President Ronald Reagan on August 20, 1987. The act established the Malcolm Baldrige National Quality Award named in honor of the former Secretary of Commerce. The Baldrige Award Criteria are considered the national standard for performance excellence. The Baldrige Award Criteria are directed toward maximizing the overall effectiveness and productivity of an organization. They are built around seven major examination categories:

- **Leadership.** Examines how the organization's senior leaders address values, directions, and performance expectations, as well as a focus on customers and other stakeholders, empowerment, innovation, and learning.
- **Strategic Planning.** Examines how the organization develops strategic objectives and action plans and how strategic objectives and action plans are deployed.
- **Customer and Market Focus.** Examines how the organization determines requirements, expectations, and customer preferences.
- **Measurement, Analysis, and Knowledge Management.** Examines how the organization selects, gathers, analyzes, manages, and improves its data, information, and knowledge assets.
- **Human Resource Focus.** Examines how the organization's work systems and employee learning and motivation enable employees to develop and use their full potential in alignment with the organization's overall objectives and action plans.
- **Process Management.** Examines the key aspects of the organization's process management, including key product, service, and business processes and key support processes.
- **Business Results.** Examines the organization's performance and improvement in key business areas, which include customer satisfaction, product/service performance, financial/marketplace performance, human resource results, operational performance, and governance/social responsibility.[6]

Baldrige Core Values and Concepts

The Baldrige core values and concepts are interrelated and run through all 88 areas in the criteria. They include:

- Visionary leadership
- Customer-driven excellence
- Organizational and personal learning
- Valuing employees and partners
- Agility
- Focus on the future
- Managing for innovation
- Management by fact
- Social responsibility
- Focus on results and creating value
- Systems perspective[7]

The Baldrige Award

The Baldrige awards are traditionally presented by the President of the United States and the Secretary of Commerce in special ceremonies in Washington, D.C. These annual awards recognize U.S. organizations that excel in performance excellence. As many as two awards may be given in each of five eligibility categories:

1. Manufacturing businesses
2. Service businesses
3. Small businesses
4. Educational organizations
5. Health care organizations[8]

A not-for-profit category will be added as a sixth eligibility category when approved by Congress.

The Baldrige Criteria

The Baldrige Criteria establish guidelines and criteria that can be used by public and private organizations to evaluate their homeland security efforts. The Baldrige Criteria can provide guidance to public and private organizations by helping them disseminate the various homeland security initiatives that are being undertaken within their organization and to identify various opportunities for improvement throughout their organization regarding homeland security issues.

The use of this manual to conduct a comprehensive organizational assessment based on Baldrige Criteria for homeland security preparedness provides an organizational perspective of their readiness and vulnerabilities that exist within their overall infrastructure.

Homeland Security Advisory System (HSAS)

A presidential directive 3 (PD-3) signed into law by President George W. Bush in March 2002 created the color-coded Homeland Security Advisory System (HSAS). The implementation of the color-coded system provides a common language and understanding for all levels of government and the general public to follow regarding critical threats to homeland security. This color-coded Advisory System ensures that homeland security warning information reaches the appropriate federal, state, local authorities, public and private organizations, including the American public, in a timely manner.[9]

1 How to Use the Baldrige Criteria and HSAS to Assess Your Organization

The alignment of the Baldrige Criteria with the color-coded Homeland Security Advisory System (HSAS) provides a unique assessment methodology for an organization to gauge its homeland security vulnerabilities and readiness in case of a major terrorist attack. Both the Baldrige Criteria and HSAS have been recognized as "best practice" initiatives for organizations to use to assess and to ensure that their performance excellence and security is competitive in the global marketplace.

An organization would want to assess itself using the Baldrige Criteria because thousands of U.S. organizations stay abreast of ever-increasing competition and improve performance excellence using this internationally recognized quality standard. The criteria help an organization align resources and approaches and improve corporate-wide communications, productivity, and effectiveness.

The Baldrige assessment scoring system is based on two evaluation dimensions: (1) process and (2) results. Each dimension should be considered before assigning a percentage score. All process evaluation dimension categories are linked to results, as well as being linked to each other. In addition, each of the categories assessed will have Homeland Security Scoring Profiles based on the Homeland Security Advisory System to help facilitate the scoring process.

Process Evaluation Dimension (Baldrige Categories 1–6)

"Process" refers to the methods your organization uses and improves to address the item requirements in Categories 1–6. The four factors used to evaluate process are approach, deployment, learning, and integration (A-D-L-I).

"Approach" (A) refers to:

- The methods used to accomplish the process.
- The appropriateness of the methods to the item requirements.
- The effectiveness of use of the methods.
- The degree to which the approach is repeatable and based on reliable data and information (i.e., systematic).

"Deployment" (D) refers to the extent to which:

- Your approach is applied in addressing item requirements relevant and important to your organization.
- Your approach is applied consistently.
- Your approach is used by all appropriate work units.

"Learning" (L) refers to:

- Refining your approach through cycles of evaluation and improvement.
- Encouraging breakthrough change to your approach through innovation.
- Sharing of refinements and innovation with other relevant work units and processes in your organization.

"Integration" (I) refers to the extent to which:

- Your approach is aligned with your organizational needs identified in other criteria item requirements.
- Your measures, information, and improvement systems are complementary across processes and work units.
- Your plans, processes, results, analysis, learning, and actions are harmonized across processes and work units to support organization-wide goals.

Results Evaluation Dimension (Baldrige Category 7)

"Results" refers to your organization's outputs and outcomes in achieving the requirements in items 7.1–7.6. The five factors used to evaluate results are performance levels, trends, comparisons, linkage, and gap (Le-T-C-Li-G).

"Performance Levels" (Le) refers to:

- Performance position of data
- Rank of data performance
- Current data performance
- Numerical information that places or positions the organization's results and performance on a meaningful measurement scale

"Trends" (T) refers to:

- Ratio (i.e., slope of trend data)
- Breadth (i.e., how widely deployed and shared)

"Comparisons" (C) refers to:

- Performance relative to appropriate comparisons
- Comparisons against exemplary results

"Linkage" (Li) refers to:

- Alignment of data to important customer product and service, process, and action plan performance requirements
- Complementary measures and results that are aligned throughout many parts of the organization
- Connective measures throughout the organization that drive key organizational strategies and goals

"Gap" (G) refers to:

- An interval in results data
- Missing segments of data

"Importance" as a Scoring Consideration

The two evaluation dimensions, described in the previous section, are critical to evaluation and feedback. However, another critical consideration in evaluation and feedback is the importance of your reported process and results to your organization's key business factors (i.e., key customer requirements, competitive environment, key strategic objectives, and action plans).

The percent scores range from a low of 0% for zero-based preparation to a high of 100% for world-class preparation. An organization can be 0% (zero-based) in some areas and 100% (world-class) in others. The anchor point is 50%, which is middle range. Many organizations fall below the 50% anchor point regarding homeland security preparation. The 50% anchor point is considered to be good, but certainly below what an organization that is striving to be the "best-in-class" in homeland security preparation among leading organizations would score.

Zero-Based Preparation   **World-Class Preparation**

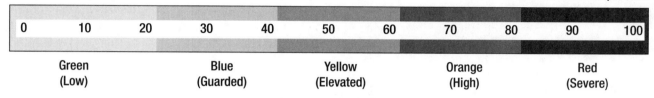

| 0 | 10 | 20 | 30 | 40 | 50 | 60 | 70 | 80 | 90 | 100 |

| Green (Low) | | Blue (Guarded) | | Yellow (Elevated) | | Orange (High) | | Red (Severe) | |

(Circle Appropriate Percentile)

Organizations that score 0% have an anecdotal approach, lack deployment, and have no meaningful results. Organizations that score 100% reflect a refined, very mature approach that is deployed and well adapted with sustainable results in all relevant areas of the organization.

BALDRIGE SCORING GUIDELINES

For use with Categories 1–6

Score	Process
0–5%	• No systematic approach is evident; information is anecdotal. (A) • Little or no deployment of an approach is evident. (D) • No evidence of an improvement orientation; improvement is achieved through reacting to problems.(L) • No organizational alignment is evident; individual areas or work units operate independently. (I)
10–25%	• The beginning of a systematic approach to the basic requirements of the Item is evident. (A) • The approach is in the early stages of deployment in most areas or work units, inhibiting progress in achieving the basic requirements of the item. (D) • Early stages of a transition from reacting to problems to a general improvement orientation are evident. (L) • The approach is aligned with other areas or work units largely through joint problem solving. (I)
30–45%	• An effective, systematic approach, responsive to the basic requirements of the item, is evident. (A) • The approach is deployed, although some areas or work units are in early stages of deployment. (D) • The beginning of a systematic approach to evaluation and improvement of key processes is evident. (L) • The approach is in early stages of alignment with your basic organizational needs identified inresponse to the other criteria categories. (I)
50–65%	• An effective, systematic approach, responsive to the overall requirements of the item, is evident. (A) • The approach is well deployed, although deployment may vary in some areas or work units. (D) • A fact-based, systematic evaluation and improvement process and some organizational learning are in place for improving the efficiency and effectiveness of key processes. (L) • The approach is aligned with your organizational needs identified in response to the other criteria categories. (I)
70–85%	• An effective, systematic approach, responsive to the multiple requirements of the item, is evident. (A) • The approach is well deployed, with no significant gaps. (D) • Fact-based, systematic evaluation and improvement and organizational learning are key management tools; there is clear evidence of refinement and innovation as a result of organizational-level analysis and sharing. (L) • The approach is integrated with your organizational needs identified in response to the other criteria items. (I)
90–100%	• An effective, systematic approach, fully responsive to the multiple requirements of the item, is evident. (A) • The approach is fully deployed without significant weaknesses or gaps in any areas or work units. (D) • Fact-based, systematic evaluation and improvement and organizational learning are key organization-wide tools; refinement and innovation, backed by analysis and sharing, are evident throughout the organization. (L) • The approach is well integrated with your organizational needs identified in response to the other criteria items. (I)

Process Evaluation Factors
A = Approach   D = Deployment   L = Learning   I = Integration

BALDRIGE SCORING GUIDELINES

For use with Category 7

Score	Process
0–5%	• There are no business results or poor results in areas reported. (Le) • Trend data are either not reported or show mainly adverse trends. (T) • Comparative information is not reported. (C) • Results are not reported for any areas of importance to your organization's key business requirements. (Li) • No results are reported for most key organizational initiatives. (G)
10–25%	• A few business results are reported; there are some improvements and/or early good performance levels in a few areas. (Le) • Little or no trend data are reported. (T) • Little or no comparative information is reported. (C) • Results are reported for a few areas of importance to your organization's key business requirements. (Li) • Limited results are reported for many organizational initiatives. (G)
30–45%	• Improvements and/or good performance levels are reported in many areas addressed in the item requirements. (Le) • Early stages of developing trends are evident. (T) • Early stages of obtaining comparative information are evident. (C) • Results are reported for many areas of importance to your organization's key business requirements. (Li) • Several results are reported with some missing segments. (G)
50–65%	• Improvement trends and/or good performance levels are reported for most areas addressed in the item requirements. (Le) • No pattern of adverse trends and no poor performance levels are evident in areas of importance to your organization's key business requirements. (T) • Some trends and/or current performance levels—evaluated against relevant comparisons and/or benchmarks—show areas of good to very good relative performance. (C) • Business results address most key customer, market, and process requirements. (Li) • Some results are missing in key areas. (G)
70–85%	• Current performance is good to excellent in most areas of importance to the Item requirements. (Le) • Most improvement trends and/or current performance levels are sustained. (T) • Many to most reported trends and/or current performance levels—evaluated against relevant comparisons and/or benchmarks—show areas of leadership and very good relative performance. (C) • Business results address most key customer, market, process, and action plan requirements. (Li) • A few results have missing segments. (G)
90–100%	• Current performance is excellent in most areas of importance to the item requirements. (Le) • Excellent improvement trends and/or sustained excellent performance levels are reported in most areas. (T) • Evidence of industry and benchmark leadership is demonstrated in many areas. (C) • Business results fully address key customer, market, process, and action plan requirements. (Li) • Most results are in place with few missing segments. (G)

Results Evaluation Factors

Le = Performance Levels   T = Trends   C = Comparisons   Li =Linkage   G = Gap

Scoring Profiles Based on Risk of Attack Levels

Scoring of the 19 Baldrige items can be difficult for an assessment team to complete. Scoring profiles based on the Homeland Security Advisory System are provided in the manual to aid the team's scoring process. The teams should first consider the two dimensions (Process and Results) and review the Baldrige Scoring Guidelines before using the Homeland Security Advisory System Risk of Attack Levels Scoring Profiles section. The scoring profiles will aid the team in further profiling and fine-tuning the percentile range in which the scores should fall.

Presidential Directives for Homeland Security

A presidential directive established the Homeland Security Advisory System to provide a comprehensive and effective means to disseminate information regarding the risk of terrorist acts to federal, state, and local authorities, to the American public, and to both public and private organizations.

The system creates a common vocabulary, context, and structure for organizations to gauge various levels of protection that are either in place or need to be installed to reduce an organization's vulnerability to various terrorist attacks.

The following threat conditions each represent an increasing risk of terrorist attacks. The Department of Homeland Security has suggested various protective measures for organizations to follow and has provided the following risk of attack level color codes:

Homeland Security Advisory System (HSAS) Risk of Attack Levels

1. **Low Condition (Green).** This condition is declared when there is a low risk of terrorist attacks. Organizations should consider the following general measures in addition to the specific protective measures they develop and implement:
   - Refining and exercising as appropriate preplanned protective measures
   - Ensuring personnel receive proper training on the Homeland Security Advisory System and specific preplanned protective measures
   - Institutionalizing a process to ensure that all facilities are regularly assessed for vulnerabilities to terrorist attacks and all reasonable measures are taken to mitigate these vulnerabilities
2. **Guarded Condition (Blue).** This condition is declared when there is a general risk of terrorist attacks. In addition to the protective measures taken in the low threat condition, organizations should consider the following general measures in addition to specific protective measures that they will develop and implement:
   - Checking communications with designated emergency response or command locations
   - Reviewing and updating emergency response procedures
   - Providing the stakeholders with any information that would strengthen their ability to act appropriately
3. **Elevated Condition (Yellow).** An elevated condition is declared when there is a significant risk of terrorist attacks. In addition to the protective measures taken in previous threat conditions, organizations should consider the following general measures in addition to the protective measures that they will develop and implement:
   - Increasing surveillance of critical locations
   - Coordinating emergency plans as appropriate
   - Assessing whether the precise characteristics of the threat require the further refinement of preplanned protective measures
   - Implementing, as appropriate, contingency and emergency response plans
4. **High Condition (Orange).** A high condition is declared when there is a high risk of terrorist attacks. In addition to the protective measures taken in the previous three conditions, organizations should consider the following general measures in addition to protective measures that they will develop and implement:

- Coordinating necessary security efforts with federal, state, and local law enforcement agencies or any National Guard or other appropriate armed forces organizations
- Taking additional precautions at public events and possibly considering alternative venues or even cancellation
- Preparing to execute contingence procedures, such as moving to an alternate site or dispersing the workforce
- Restricting threatened facility access to essential personnel only

5. **Severe Condition (Red).** A Severe Condition reflects a severe risk of terrorist attacks. Under most circumstances, the protective measures for a severe condition are not intended to be sustained for substantial periods of time. In addition to the protective measures in the previous threat conditions, organizations should consider the following general measures in addition to specific protective measures that they will develop and implement:
   - Increasing or redirecting personnel to address critical emergency needs
   - Assigning emergency response personnel and prepositioning and mobilizing specially trained teams or resources
   - Monitoring, redirecting, or constraining transportation systems
   - Closing public facilities

Assessment Scores Based on Risk of Attack Levels

Homeland Security Scoring Profiles based on the Homeland Security Advisory System have been developed for the assessment team to use to better gauge their organization's level of preparedness for a major terrorist attack. The higher the score for each question reflects the organization's level of preparation for homeland security.

An organization may score in lower percentile color levels within some areas of the assessment. All scores should be aligned with the organizations strategic and business needs that are related to homeland security.

Based on the organization's homeland security needs, it may not be appropriate or cost effective for an organization to consistently score in the upper levels for each question within the assessment. The assessment teams should always refer to their **organizational overview** before assigning a percentile score. After referring to the **organizational overview,** the assessment team(s) should first review the **Baldrige Scoring Guidelines** before reviewing the **Homeland Security Scoring Profiles** listed in this chapter.

The Baldrige Scoring Guidelines should always be considered first by the teams when scoring and then the team(s) should validate their score against the Homeland Security Scoring Profiles to ensure that together both the Baldrige Scoring Guidelines and the Homeland Security Scoring Profiles adequately describe the organization's homeland security preparedness level that each question addresses throughout the assessment.

HOMELAND SECURITY SCORING PROFILES

(Based on Homeland Security Advisory System. Baldrige Categories are profiled into five percentile ranges.)

World-Class
Preparation

1. Leadership

SEVERE
(Red)
80–100%

- Senior leadership is visibly involved in promoting homeland security.
- Senior leaders promote the formation of employee teams throughout the organization to focus on homeland security.
- Senior leadership reflects the organization's commitment to public health, safety, and environmental protection.
- Homeland security planning is promoted by senior leaders and integrated throughout the organization.

HIGH
(Orange)
60–80%

- Most senior leaders promote homeland security initiatives among employees.
- Senior leadership meets with employee teams, key suppliers, partners, and customers on homeland security issues.
- Leadership at all levels promotes homeland security as a major priority for the organization.
- Homeland security plan is integral to all senior leaders and managers performance review.

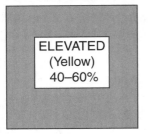

ELEVATED
(Yellow)
40–60%

- Senior leadership shares corporate values regarding homeland security priorities with employees, customers, partners, and suppliers.
- Senior leadership is committed to public responsibility and corporate leadership regarding homeland security.
- Senior leaders support short- and long-term strategic planning for homeland security.
- Homeland security plan is integrated into all senior leaders' performance reviews.

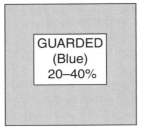

GUARDED
(Blue)
20–40%

- A few senior leaders and managers support and are involved in the organization's homeland security efforts.
- Homeland security initiatives exist in some parts of the organization.
- Organization's corporate policies and procedures reflect some commitment to homeland security
- Homeland security plan is promoted by some senior leaders.

LOW
(Green)
0–20%

- Some leaders are beginning to support organizational involvement in homeland security initiatives.
- Senior leadership does not get involved with employees, suppliers, partners, and customers regarding homeland security issues and concerns.
- Senior leadership does not have a homeland security plan in place.
- Homeland security plan is promoted only by senior leaders.

Zero-Based Preparation

Risk of Attack Levels

Process Dimension (Categories 1–6)
Evaluation Factors

☑ **Approach** (methods used to accomplish the process)

☑ **Deployment** (application of the approach throughout the organization)

☑ **Learning** (refinement of the approach through cycles of evaluation)

☑ **Integration** (alignment of the approach throughout the organization)

HOMELAND SECURITY SCORING PROFILES

(Based on Homeland Security Advisory System. Baldrige Categories are profiled into five percentile ranges.)

World-Class
Preparation

2. Strategic Planning

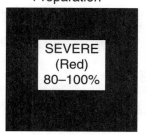

**SEVERE
(Red)
80–100%**

- Organization's strategic planning process includes homeland security initiatives.
- Organization seeks and receives homeland security input from employees, suppliers, partners, and customers before developing a strategic plan.
- The strategic planning process for homeland security includes short- and longer-term plans based on key security data, customer, supplier, partner, and employee survey data, and benchmark data deployed throughout the organization.
- Homeland security is a critical component of the organization's strategic plans and goals.

**HIGH
(Orange)
60–80%**

- Senior management provides homeland security input and approves the strategic plan.
- Operational homeland security plans linked to the master strategic plan are developed throughout the organization.
- Managers are held accountable for meeting strategic homeland security goals and objectives.
- Homeland security initiatives are aligned throughout the strategic planning process.

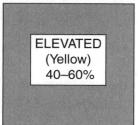

**ELEVATED
(Yellow)
40–60%**

- Operational homeland security plans developed at departmental levels link with master plan.
- Organization involves employees, suppliers, partners, and customers in homeland security planning process.
- Managers at all levels are held accountable for meeting homeland security goals and objectives.
- Homeland security strategic goals and plans initiatives are beginning to be better aligned throughout the organization.

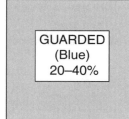

**GUARDED
(Blue)
20–40%**

- Strategic homeland security goals are established for key functional areas of the organization.
- Some employees, suppliers, partners, and customers are involved in the homeland security strategic planning.
- Some senior managers are involved in homeland security planning.
- Some strategic alignment of homeland security initiatives within the organization is evident.

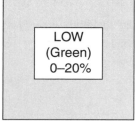

**LOW
(Green)
0–20%**

- None to very few employees, suppliers, partners, and customers are involved in planning for homeland security.
- Homeland security planning is not included in the organization's strategic planning process.
- Employees beyond senior managers are not involved in planning for homeland security.
- No organizational alignment is evident for homeland security strategic initiatives.

Risk of Attack Levels

Zero-Based Preparation

Process Dimension (Categories 1–6)
Evaluation Factors

☑ **Approach** (methods used to accomplish the process)

☑ **Deployment** (application of the approach throughout the organization)

☑ **Learning** (refinement of the approach through cycles of evaluation)

☑ **Integration** (alignment of the approach throughout the organization)

HOMELAND SECURITY SCORING PROFILES

(Based on Homeland Security Advisory System. Baldrige Categories are profiled into five percentile ranges.)

3. Customer and Market Focus

World-Class Preparation

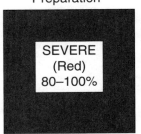
SEVERE
(Red)
80–100%

- Organization conducts surveys, focus groups, and exit interviews to determine customer requirements for homeland security.
- Organization promotes trust and confidence in its products/services to customers regarding homeland security.
- Organization is continuously gauging customer and market requirements and expectations regarding homeland security issues.
- Homeland security is totally integrated with customer service initiatives.

HIGH
(Orange)
60–80%

- Effective feedback systems are in place to obtain critical customer and market data regarding homeland security.
- Customer-contact employees are given homeland security training.
- Logistical support is in place for customers to provide homeland security support.
- Homeland security issues are aligned with customer service initiatives.

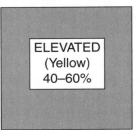
ELEVATED
(Yellow)
40–60%

- Effective customer support regarding homeland security is in place.
- A complaint management process for customer concerns regarding homeland security is in place.
- Customer-contact employees are trained on homeland security issues.
- Homeland security issues are partially aligned with customer service initiatives.

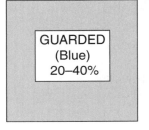
GUARDED
(Blue)
20–40%

- Most customer groups and markets are segmented regarding homeland security requirements.
- Customer follow-up system is in place to address homeland security issues.
- Future homeland security expectations and requirements are determined and considered for future implementation among many customers.
- Homeland security is beginning to be aligned with customer initiatives.

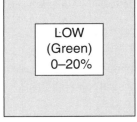
LOW
(Green)
0–20%

- Organization does not consistently promote trust and confidence with customers regarding homeland security issues.
- Organization does not survey its customers/markets regarding homeland security issues.
- Organization does not consider homeland security a customer service issue.
- Homeland security is not integrated into customer service initiatives.

Risk of Attack Levels

Zero-Based Preparation

Process Dimension (Categories 1–6)
Evaluation Factors

[✔] **Approach** (methods used to accomplish the process)

[✔] **Deployment** (application of the approach throughout the organization)

[✔] **Learning** (refinement of the approach through cycles of evaluation)

[✔] **Integration** (alignment of the approach throughout the organization)

HOMELAND SECURITY SCORING PROFILES

(Based on Homeland Security Advisory System. Baldrige Categories are profiled into five percentile ranges.)

World-Class
Preparation

4. Measurement, Analysis, and Knowledge Management

**SEVERE
(Red)
80–100%**

- Processes and technology to ensure timely, accurate, valid, and useful homeland security data for employees, suppliers, partners, and customers are in place.
- Competitive comparisons and benchmarking information and data are used to improve and maintain homeland security.
- Homeland security data are analyzed organization-wide by employee teams that translate it into useful information to help secure the workplace environment.
- Homeland security knowledge and data are measured and deployed throughout the organization.

**HIGH
(Orange)
60–80%**

- Employees have rapid access to homeland security data throughout the organization.
- Comparative homeland security data are collected, analyzed, and translated into useful information to support a secure workplace.
- Processes and technologies are used across most of the organization to ensure that homeland security data are complete, timely, accurate, valid, and useful.
- Homeland security data are integrated with daily operations.

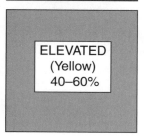

**ELEVATED
(Yellow)
40–60%**

- Employees have access to homeland security data in many parts of the organization.
- Most critical processes have homeland security data that are complete, accurate, and timely.
- Measures exist that gauge homeland security effectiveness throughout the organization.
- Homeland security data are measured, analyzed, and distributed throughout most of the organization.

**GUARDED
(Blue)
20–40%**

- Homeland security data exist for some critical products/services and processes.
- Organization ensures that hardware and software are reliable, secure, and user-friendly regarding homeland security.
- Homeland security data and knowledge are transferred to key customers, suppliers, and partners.
- Homeland security data and knowledge are beginning to be aligned throughout the organization.

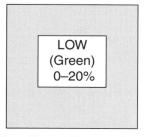

**LOW
(Green)
0–20%**

- Homeland security data received for comparison appear anecdotal.
- Limited homeland security data are used to ensure a secure workplace for employees.
- Collection of homeland security data is in the beginning stages within the organization and not consistently shared with customers, suppliers, and partners.
- Homeland security data and knowledge are not integrated throughout the organization.

Zero-Based Preparation

Risk of Attack Levels

Process Dimension (Categories 1–6)
Evaluation Factors

☑ **Approach** (methods used to accomplish the process)

☑ **Deployment** (application of the approach throughout the organization)

☑ **Learning** (refinement of the approach through cycles of evaluation)

☑ **Integration** (alignment of the approach throughout the organization)

HOMELAND SECURITY SCORING PROFILES

(Based on Homeland Security Advisory System. Baldrige Categories are profiled into five percentile ranges.)

World-Class
Preparation

5. Human Resource Focus

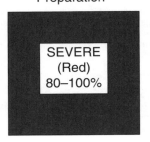

**SEVERE
(Red)
80–100%**

- Organization is highly sensitive to employee well-being and satisfaction regarding homeland security.
- Organization supports homeland security plans and goals through employee education, training, and development initiatives.
- Organization supports workplace preparedness for emergencies and homeland security by promoting cross-functional teams to address and to be recognized for innovative problem-solving approaches in identifying and resolving homeland security issues.
- Homeland security issues are totally integrated within the organization's workforce initiatives.

**HIGH
(Orange)
60–80%**

- Senior and middle management support and recognize employee involvement, contributions, and teamwork in resolving homeland security issues.
- Employee idea sharing and innovation is encouraged regarding homeland security.
- Employees are empowered and rewarded when they identify and address homeland security issues.
- Homeland security is integrated with most of the organization's workforce initiatives.

**ELEVATED
(Yellow)
40–60%**

- Homeland security awareness is promoted within many parts of the organization.
- Employees are given homeland security training on an annual basis.
- Management supports cross-functional teams to identify homeland security opportunities for the organization.
- Homeland security issues are partially integrated with the organization's workforce initiatives.

**GUARDED
(Blue)
20–40%**

- Managers in some parts of the organization support employee involvement in homeland security.
- Organization does not consistently keep employees informed regarding homeland security issues.
- Employee training initiatives do not consistently address homeland security issues.
- Homeland security is integrated with some workforce training and safety issues.

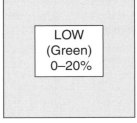

**LOW
(Green)
0–20%**

- Few employees within the organization are empowered to work on homeland security issues.
- Workforce is rarely surveyed regarding its well-being and satisfaction with the organization's homeland security initiatives.
- Employees involved with improving homeland security are seldom recognized by the organization.
- Homeland security is not aligned with workforce issues and a safework environment.

Zero-Based Preparation

Risk of Attack Levels

Process Dimension (Categories 1–6)
Evaluation Factors

☑ **Approach** (methods used to accomplish the process)

☑ **Deployment** (application of the approach throughout the organization)

☑ **Learning** (refinement of the approach through cycles of evaluation)

☑ **Integration** (alignment of the approach throughout the organization)

HOMELAND SECURITY SCORING PROFILES

(Based on Homeland Security Advisory System. Baldrige Categories are profiled into five percentile ranges.)

World-Class Preparation

Risk of Attack Levels

6. Process Management

SEVERE (Red) 80–100%

- Key homeland security processes have been identified and documented across the organization.
- Systematic approaches are used to document key homeland security processes to ensure shortened cycle time and consistent procedures.
- Critical homeland security processes are reviewed on an ongoing basis to reduce variability and to keep the processes current with homeland security needs and directions.
- Homeland security initiatives are aligned with key customer, supplier, and partner process initiatives.

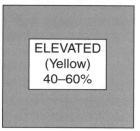

HIGH (Orange) 60–80%

- Key homeland security processes are documented and controlled across the organization.
- Comprehensive homeland security assessments are conducted throughout the organization on an annual basis.
- Analytic problem-solving tools are used within the organization to identify and solve homeland security problems.
- Homeland security issues are aligned with the organization's key business processes.

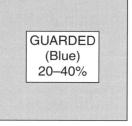

ELEVATED (Yellow) 40–60%

- Process assessments are conducted in many parts of the organization to ensure a safe work environment.
- Customer, supplier, partner, and employee survey results are used to gauge homeland security readiness.
- Organization identifies and documents key processes that support homeland security.
- Homeland security issues are mostly aligned with the organization's key business processes.

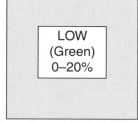

GUARDED (Blue) 20–40%

- Homeland security assessments are conducted only when a breach of security has occurred.
- Not all critical homeland security issues have been identified and addressed.
- Limited customer, supplier, and partner input is incorporated into documentation of homeland security process designs.
- Homeland security issues are partially integrated with the organization's operations and key business and support processes.

LOW (Green) 0–20%

- Organization is in an appraisal mode rather than a prevention mode regarding its assessment of homeland security issues.
- Limited homeland security assessments are conducted.
- Homeland security issues to ensure a safe work environment are seldom addressed and documented.
- Homeland security issues are not integrated with the organization's operations and key processes.

Zero-Based Preparation

Process Dimension (Categories 1–6)
Evaluation Factors

☑ **Approach** (methods used to accomplish the process)

☑ **Deployment** (application of the approach throughout the organization)

☑ **Learning** (refinement of the approach through cycles of evaluation)

☑ **Integration** (alignment of the approach throughout the organization)

HOMELAND SECURITY SCORING PROFILES

(Based on Homeland Security Advisory System. Baldrige Categories are profiled into five percentile ranges.)

Risk of Attack Levels

World-Class Preparation

SEVERE
(Red)
80–100%

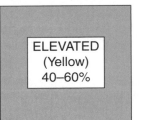

HIGH
(Orange)
60–80%

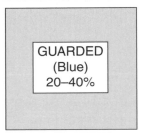

ELEVATED
(Yellow)
40–60%

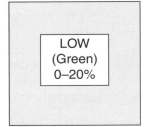

GUARDED
(Blue)
20–40%

LOW
(Green)
0–20%

Zero-Based Preparation

7. Business Results

- Customer satisfaction results regarding homeland security initiatives have shown positive results over the past three years.
- Homeland security performance results have experienced a steady improvement over the past five years.
- Employee suggestions for homeland security improvement and innovative safe work practices show positive trends over the past several years.
- Homeland security results are trended and used to align overall corporate security.

- Organization's homeland security improvement results reflect improvement in cycle time and operational performance.
- Key measures of the organization's homeland security processes reflect cycle time reductions, and cost results have improved over the past two to three years in most parts of the organization.
- Comparative homeland security benchmark results reveal that the organization is leading its industry.
- Homeland security results are used to gauge vulnerability issues throughout the organization.

- Key measures of homeland security within operations, shipping, and customer contact reflect a three-year trend of positive results.
- Supplier partnership with organization's homeland security efforts show positive trends over the past two years.
- Customer involvement with homeland security issues reflects positive results over the past two years.
- Homeland security results are mostly collected and used to gauge vulnerability issues.

- Customer satisfaction with homeland security shows positive results and trends.
- Employee involvement in homeland security projects has shown positive results over the past two years.
- Employee satisfaction with organization's homeland security effort shows positive trends over the past three years.
- Homeland security results are partially collected and deployed.

- Limited homeland security benchmark results are collected by the organization.
- Employee satisfaction with homeland security within the organization has limited results and appears to be decreasing.
- Organization's improvement in homeland security efforts appears anecdotal and has limited results.
- Homeland security results are not reported or aligned with other organizational initiatives.

Results Dimension (Category 7)
Evaluation Factors

✔ **Performance Levels** (position of data performance)

✔ **Trends** (rate and breadth of data)

✔ **Comparisons** (results relative to appropriate benchmarks)

✔ **Linkage** (alignment of data with key organizational initiatives)

✔ **Gap** (missing segments of data)

2 How to Use the Manual

How to Use the Homeland Security Manual

This manual is designed to serve as an easy-to-use guide for an organization's cross-functional self-assessment team(s) to assess and score its homeland security readiness.

This manual can be used to provide a security check due diligence for an organization's homeland security efforts, to help its employees understand what Baldrige Criteria are asking, and to provide a template for its self-assessment and strategic planning efforts regarding homeland security. In addition the manual provides guidance for employees and employee teams to score their departments or total organization in 88 areas and serves as an annual benchmark for homeland security improvement and a strategic planning guide for short-term and longer-term homeland security planning. The manual assists employees in determining their organization's readiness in case of a mass terrorist attack. The manual can also be used to help employees collect homeland security data to benchmark against other "best practice" organizations and to ultimately develop a homeland security plan.

How to Begin and Prepare for an Assessment

The assessment of an oganization should begin with the full support and sponsorship of the senior leadership. The senior leadership should appoint a homeland security assessment team administrator.

The first step in preparing for the assessment should include conducting a homeland security assessment briefing for senior leadership. This session can be conducted by the organization's safety/security division or the person who has been selected by senior leadership as the assessment team administrator to lead the assessment process. The person(s) responsible for the briefing should review this manual and have a thorough understanding of homeland security issues and the Baldrige Criteria before conducting the session.

In addition, senior leadership must be educated in homeland security issues and the principles of Baldrige Criteria to appreciate the value of conducting the assessment. Several activities are recommended to help senior leaders develop an understanding of homeland security issues and Baldrige Criteria. These include the following:

- Reading books and articles on homeland security issues (a suggested resource list is included in this manual)
- Reviewing the Malcolm Baldrige National Quality Award Criteria (included throughout this manual)
- Benchmarking other public/private organizations to review best practices (see Appendix B)

After senior leaders have been briefed, the assessment team administrator should begin the process of soliciting assessment team members. Many organizations solicit members through their corporate newsletter, electronic mail, or a personal letter sent from the president/CEO inviting participation. Team members selections should be considered from a group of employees who have expressed an interest in better understanding homeland security and using the Baldrige Criteria as a template for improving their organization's homeland security infrastructure.

Once team members have been selected, it is recommended that an assessment workshop be conducted by the assessment team administrator or team participants who have an understanding of homeland security issues and the Baldrige Criteria. The workshop may include using a case study for the team to practice identifying organizational strengths and opportunities for improvement in at least one or two categories (see http://www.baldrige.org for case study). During the workshop, the team will discuss each category and determine "What does this mean for my organization?" The use of this manual will help the team practice translating homeland security issues and Baldrige Criteria into simple language for their own organization-wide assessment.

Assessing the Organization

Team Member Selection

Assessment team members should represent a cross section of employees. All departments throughout the organization should be represented on the teams. Diversity adds value and strength to each assessment team.

In larger organizations, seven homeland security assessment/Baldrige category subteams would need to be developed. A subject matter expert (SME) for a particular Baldrige category should be selected as the category team leader. In smaller organizations where there are a limited number of personnel who could serve on assessment teams, all categories can be assessed by one team. Following are some sample assessment team compositions:

ASSESSMENT TEAM COMPOSITION (LARGE ORGANIZATION)
(20 to 50 Members)

Team 1
Leadership

- CEO, President, or Senior VP *(Team Leader)*
- Director of Legal
- Director of Public Policy
- Manager of Operations
- Customer
- Supplier
- Partner

Team 2
Strategic Planning

- VP, Strategic Planning *(Team Leader)*
- Director
- Manager
- Supervisor
- Customer
- Supplier
- Partner

Team 3
Customer and Market Focus

- VP, Marketing *(Team Leader)*
- Director
- Manager
- Supervisor
- Customer
- Supplier
- Partner

Team 4
Measurement, Analysis, and Knowledge Management

- VP, IT *(Team Leader)*
- Director of IT
- Manager
- Supervisor
- Customer
- Supplier
- Partner

Team 5
Human Resource Focus

- VP, Human Resources *(Team Leader)*
- Director
- Manager
- Supervisor
- Customer
- Supplier
- Partner

Continued

Team 6
Process Management

- VP, Operations *(Team Leader)*
- Director
- Manager
- Supervisor
- Customer
- Supplier
- Partner

Team 7
Business Results

- VP, Strategic Planning *(Team Leader)*
- Director
- Manager
- Supervisor
- Customer
- Supplier
- Partner

Note: Some teams may decide to assess only selected categories within their organization that appear vulnerable to terrorist attacks or weak in deploying homeland security initiatives. This manual allows for complete flexibility regarding the extent to which an organization conducts its assessment.

ASSESSMENT TEAM COMPOSITION (SMALL ORGANIZATION) (6 to 8 Members)

Team Assesses All Seven Baldrige Categories

- President/CEO or Senior VP *(Team Leader)*
- Director
- Manager
- Supervisor
- Customer
- Supplier/Partner

Pre-Assessment Meeting for Each Team

Each team will need to hold a pre-assessment planning meeting to identify individuals to be interviewed during the assessment. Dates and interview times need to be agreed upon during this session, and an agenda and timetable should be prepared. After the team selects the individuals within the organization to be interviewed, a team member needs to contact all persons to be interviewed.

Coordination of Assessment Team Schedules

The assessment team administrator should coordinate all seven category team schedules with team members and develop an overall assessment plan and timetable. This schedule and timetable should then be submitted to the senior leadership of the organization for review and approval.

Team Interview of Selected Participants

After approval has been secured from senior leadership, each team is ready to begin its interview process with selected participants. The entire category team will take turns interviewing the participants. This allows for more interaction and input for the assessment team. During the interview process, all assessment team members will have a copy of this manual in hand and will make notes under each of the questions. Each category team may choose to interview two to three groups of participants representing various levels throughout the organization. Interviewing hints and tips are provided in Appendix D.

Assessment Team Consensus and Scoring of the Category

After all category interviews have been completed, the category team leaders will hold a consensus review meeting in which all team members will review the findings regarding areas identified as strengths and opportunities for improvement. The team will reach a consensus and assign each item a percentile score and will ultimately award the category a total point score. A quick and easy organizational assessment for the organization's suppliers, partners, and customers is provided (see Appendix A) to help determine to what extent supplier and customer organizations have approached and deployed homeland security initiatives within their own organizations. This quick assessment may also be used as a preliminary analysis of one's own organization or to benchmark another organization's homeland security progress.

Entire Assessment Report Consolidated and Delivered

All seven category teams will deliver their assessment to the assessment team administrator. The assessment team administrator will meet with all category team leaders to review results. After the assessment team administrator and all seven category team leaders have reached a consensus on the strengths, opportunities for improvement, homeland security planning issues, category percentile scores, and the overall assessment point score, the assessment is finalized and a homeland security plan is developed. The completed assessment and homeland security plan is then delivered to the president/CEO and the other senior staff members. The entire assessment process can take as little as two weeks or as much as one month to complete.

Organizational Overview

(Complete before conducting homeland security assessment)

Assessment Review dates: _____ to _____

1.0   Organizational Policies and Procedures

  1.1   Does your organization have a published vision, mission, and statement of values for homeland security?

  Yes ☐   No ☐

  1.2   Does your organization have an organizational chart that highlights key homeland security positions?

  Yes ☐   No ☐

  1.3   Does your organization have a published overview for homeland security initiatives?

  Yes ☐   No ☐

  (If answers are yes, collect statements, organization charts, history, and overviews.)

2.0   Project Improvement Teams for Homeland Security Initiatives

  2.1   Total employee population: _____

  2.2   Project teams

Name of Project Team	Employee Projects			Functional Area Team (Check Area)						
	Hours	Number of Participants	Date of Project Completion	Sales & Marketing Distribution	Human Resources	Production Engineering/ Maintenance	Finance/ Accounting	Adminis- tration	Shipping/ Receiving	Other

3.0 Customers/Suppliers/Partners

3.1 List key customers   Number of key customers_____

Key Customer Names	Date Customer Relationship Began	Length of Time as a Customer	Unique Homeland Security Requirements

3.2 List key suppliers/partners   Number of key suppliers/partners_____

Key Supplier/ Partner Names	Date Partnership Began	Length of Time as a Supplier/ Partner	Unique Homeland Security Requirements

4.0   Homeland Security Activities

List other homeland security activities that may have been carried out in your organization during this assessment review period.

Activity	Objective

5.0   Homeland Security Training

5.1   Does your organization have a training budget for homeland security?

Yes ☐   No ☐   If no, go to 6.0.

5.2   What was your annual training expenditure for homeland security during this assessment review period?

5.3   Provide a list of homeland security training presented to employees by the organization during this assessment review period.

Internal and External Courses and Workshops	Hours	Number of Participants	Date of Training	Functional Area Team (Check Area)						
				Sales & Marketing Distribution	Human Resources	Production Engineering/ Maintenance	Finance/ Accounting	Adminis- tration	Shipping/ Receiving	Other

6.0   Homeland Security Assessments

6.1   Does your organization conduct homeland security assessments?

Yes ☐   No ☐

(If yes, please specify the areas and frequency of the assessment being conducted during this review period.)

Areas	Frequency
Internal Assessments	
External Assessments	
Others	

7.0   Trends/Improvements for Homeland Security

7.1   Are trends of key homeland security initiatives being tracked regularly?

Yes ☐   No ☐

(If yes, list and collect documents.)

Documents	How often tracked?

7.1   What are your organizational challenges regarding homeland security?

Organizational Challenges

Competitive Environment

Strategic Challenges

Performance Challenges

Notes

Eight Steps for Successful Assessment Implementation and Manual Use

The following eight steps will further explain how this manual will be useful in simplifying the assessment process for the organization.

Step One   Complete the Organizational Overview

The assessment team administrator and senior staff should complete the organizational overview (pages 23–27) before the team(s) conduct the homeland security assessment. The organizational overview is the most appropriate starting point for the assessment and will provide a snapshot of the organization's homeland security initiatives before the team(s) begins the assessment process. The information collected in the organizational overview should be used to identify potential homeland security issues and challenges. In addition, it may be used for an initial self-assessment.

Step Two   Read Baldrige Criteria

After the team or teams have been formed, members should read the Baldrige Award Criteria that appear at the beginning of each item throughout this manual. Under each item summary, the Baldrige Criteria appear under the heading *Areas to Address.*

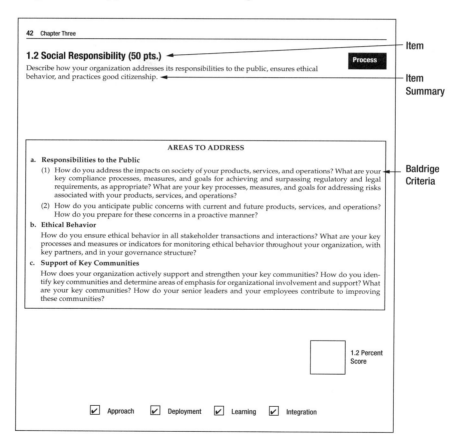

Step Three   Review Questions

Following the Areas to Address pages of the manual are homeland security questions based on the Baldrige Criteria. This manual takes all Baldrige Criteria and breaks them down into simple questions so they are more understandable and user-friendly. This allows a clearer and more precise homeland security assessment to be conducted.

The questions are to be asked to different levels of employees throughout the organization. The assessment team should divide this task among its members.

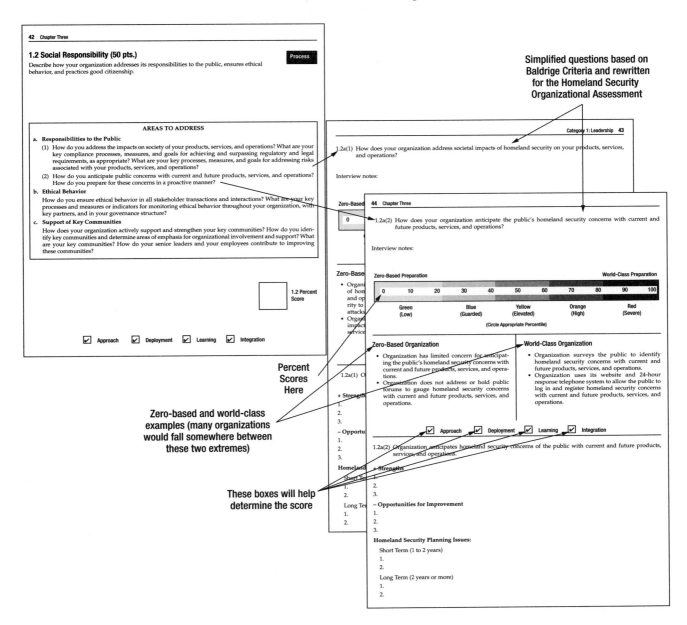

Simplified questions based on Baldrige Criteria and rewritten for the Homeland Security Organizational Assessment

Percent Scores Here

Zero-based and world-class examples (many organizations would fall somewhere between these two extremes)

These boxes will help determine the score

The Baldrige Criteria notes have been eliminated but are incorporated into the simplified questions throughout the manual.

Step Four   Zero-Based and World-Class

Before recording answers to the questions, review the examples of zero-based and world-class organizations' homeland security initiatives that appear in the center of the page.

Below the examples appear four boxes labeled Approach, Deployment, Learning, and Integration. These boxes will aid in assessing the kinds of information and/or data the question requires. (Refer to Chapter 1.)

Step Five   Make Interview Notes

Near the top of the page under each question is an interview notes section for recording answers to the questions given by employees as they are being interviewed by the assessment team. This data should be used to determine strengths, opportunities, and homeland security strategic planning issues located in the lower portion of the page.

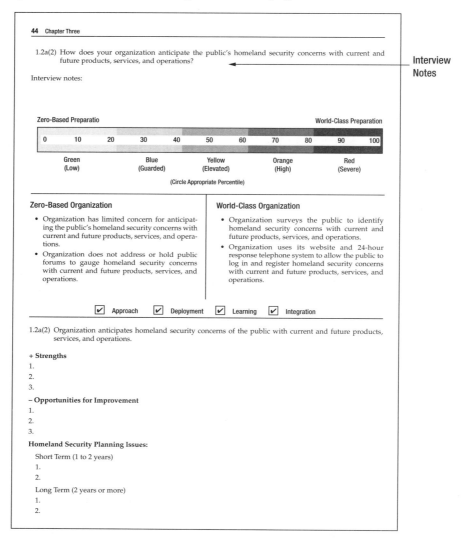

Step Six   List Comments for Strengths and Improvement

On the lower half of the page, the question is restated. After the interviews are completed, review the interview notes. The team will then list strengths and opportunities for improvement. All comments should be written in short, complete sentences.

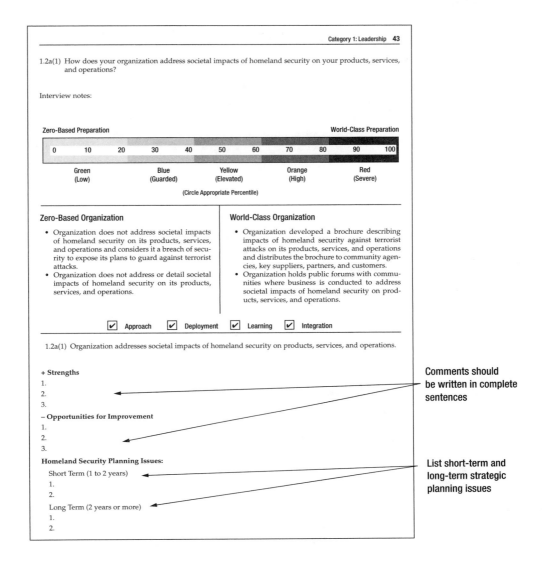

1.2a(1) How does your organization address societal impacts of homeland security on your products, services, and operations?

Interview notes:

Zero-Based Preparation   World-Class Preparation

| 0 | 10 | 20 | 30 | 40 | 50 | 60 | 70 | 80 | 90 | 100 |

Green   Blue   Yellow   Orange   Red
(Low)   (Guarded)   (Elevated)   (High)   (Severe)

(Circle Appropriate Percentile)

Zero-Based Organization

- Organization does not address societal impacts of homeland security on its products, services, and operations and considers it a breach of security to expose its plans to guard against terrorist attacks.
- Organization does not address or detail societal impacts of homeland security on its products, services, and operations.

World-Class Organization

- Organization developed a brochure describing impacts of homeland security against terrorist attacks on its products, services, and operations and distributes the brochure to community agencies, key suppliers, partners, and customers.
- Organization holds public forums with communities where business is conducted to address societal impacts of homeland security on products, services, and operations.

☑ Approach   ☑ Deployment   ☑ Learning   ☑ Integration

1.2a(1) Organization addresses societal impacts of homeland security on products, services, and operations.

+ Strengths
1.
2.
3.
– Opportunities for Improvement
1.
2.
3.
Homeland Security Planning Issues:
Short Term (1 to 2 years)
1.
2.
Long Term (2 years or more)
1.
2.

Comments should be written in complete sentences

List short-term and long-term strategic planning issues

Step Seven   List Homeland Security Strategic Planning Issues

After reviewing the interview notes, strengths, and opportunities for improvement, the assessment team should list any short-term and long-term strategic planning issues. These data can be used later when developing a homeland security strategic plan for the organization. Homeland security plan and budget forms are available on the CD-ROM included with this manual.

Step Eight   Score Assessment Items

The assessment is broken down into seven Baldrige categories:

1. Leadership
2. Strategic Planning
3. Customer and Market Focus
4. Measurement, Analysis, and Knowledge Management
5. Human Resource Focus
6. Process Management
7. Business Results

These seven categories are divided into 19 assessment items (i.e., 1.1, 1.2, 2.1, 2.2, . . .) and the 19 assessment items are broken down into 88 areas (i.e., 1.1a(1), 1.1b, . . .). The percent score is reflective of the strengths and opportunities for improvement of the areas within each assessment item. Thus, throughout the assessment, all 19 items will obtain a percent score. All assessment item percent scores will be transferred to the Summary of Assessment Items for Homeland Security score sheet located at the end of Chapter 9. A graph illustrating the hierarchy of organizational homeland security scores, based on Baldrige Criteria, visually presents the percent scores of each assessment category.

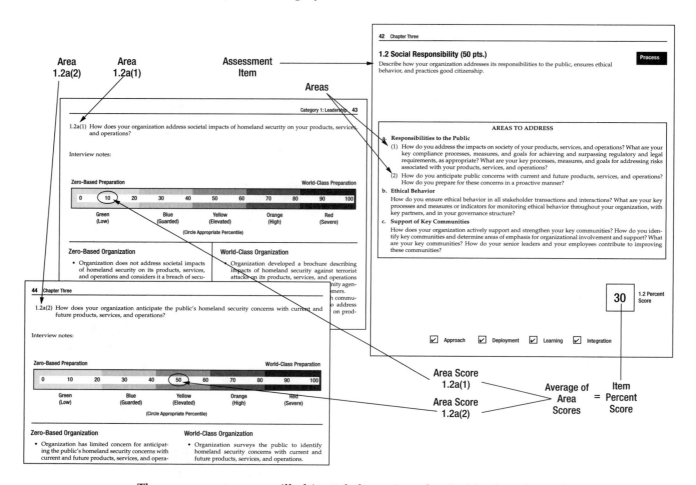

The assessment scores will ultimately be reviewed, prioritized, and transformed into actionable strategies for homeland security improvement, and a homeland security plan can be developed. The transformation process for consolidating homeland security assessment findings into a homeland security plan is explained in detail in Chapter 10 of the manual. All assessment documents featured in this manual are available from the CD-ROM included inside the back cover.

3 Category 1 Leadership

1 Leadership (120 pts.)[10]

The Leadership category examines how the organization's senior leaders address values, directions, and performance expectations, as well as a focus on customers and other stakeholders, empowerment, innovation, and learning regarding the organization's homeland security initiatives. Also examined are the organization's governance and how the organization addresses its public and community responsibilities for homeland security.

 Forms can be downloaded from the CD-ROM located inside the back cover of this book.

1.1 Organizational Leadership (70 pts.)

Describe how senior leaders guide your organization. Describe your organization's governance system. Describe how senior leaders review organizational performance.

AREAS TO ADDRESS

a. Senior Leadership Direction

(1) How do senior leaders set and deploy organizational values, short- and longer-term directions, and performance expectations? How do senior leaders include a focus on creating and balancing value for customers and other stakeholders in their performance expectations? How do senior leaders communicate organizational values, directions, and expectations through your leadership system, to all employees, and to key suppliers and partners? How do senior leaders ensure two-way communication on these topics?

(2) How do senior leaders create an environment for empowerment, innovation, and organizational agility? How do they create an environment for organizational and employee learning? How do they create an environment that fosters and requires legal and ethical behavior?

b. Organizational Governance

How does your organization address the following key factors in your governance system?

- Management accountability for the organization's actions
- Fiscal accountability
- Independence in internal and external audits
- Protection of stockholder and stakeholder interests, as appropriate

c. Organizational Performance Review

(1) How do senior leaders review organizational performance and capabilities? How do they use these reviews to assess organizational success, competitive performance, and progress relative to short- and longer-term foals? How do they use these reviews to assess your organizational ability to address changing organizational needs?

(2) What are the key performance measures regularly reviewed by your senior leaders? What are your key recent performance review findings?

(3) How do senior leaders translate organizational performance review findings into priorities for continuous and breakthrough improvement of key business results and into opportunities for innovation? How are these priorities and opportunities deployed throughout your organization? When appropriate, how are they deployed to your suppliers and partners to ensure organizational alignment?

(4) How do you evaluate the performance of your senior leaders, including the chief executive? How do you evaluate the performance of members of the board of directors, as appropriate? How do senior leaders use organizational performance review findings to improve both their own leadership effectiveness and that of your board and leadership system, as appropriate?

1.1 Percent Score

☑ Approach   ☑ Deployment   ☑ Learning   ☑ Integration

1.1a(1) How do your senior leaders set and deploy organizational values, short- and longer-term directions, and performance expectations as they relate to homeland security within the organization?

Interview notes:

Zero-Based Preparation　　　　　　　　　　　　　　　　　　　　**World-Class Preparation**

0	10	20	30	40	50	60	70	80	90	100

Green (Low)	Blue (Guarded)	Yellow (Elevated)	Orange (High)	Red (Severe)

(Circle Appropriate Percentile)

Zero-Based Organization

- A limited number of senior leaders are involved in setting and deploying homeland security directions and expectations among the workforce.
- Senior leaders outsource all management of the organization's homeland security directions and expectations to outside consultants.

World-Class Organization

- Senior leaders are personally involved in setting and deploying homeland security directions and expectations throughout the organization.
- Senior leaders volunteer with citizen corps in the communities where the organization is located and deploy corporate security values among employees, customers, partners, and suppliers.

☑ Approach　　☑ Deployment　　☑ Learning　　☑ Integration

1.1a(1) Senior leaders set and deploy organizational values, short- and longer-term directions, and performance expectations as they relate to homeland security within the organization.

+ Strengths

1.
2.
3.

– Opportunities for Improvement

1.
2.
3.

Homeland Security Planning Issues:

Short Term (1 to 2 years)

1.
2.

Long Term (2 years or more)

1.
2.

1.1a(2) How do your senior leaders create an environment for empowerment, innovation, and organizational agility among employees regarding homeland security issues throughout the organization?

Interview notes:

Zero-Based Preparation   **World-Class Preparation**

0	10	20	30	40	50	60	70	80	90	100

Green	Blue	Yellow	Orange	Red
(Low)	(Guarded)	(Elevated)	(High)	(Severe)

(Circle Appropriate Percentile)

Zero-Based Organization

- Senior leaders do not encourage employees to discuss homeland security issues on the job.
- Senior leaders are not concerned about employee involvement in emergency readiness, and they forbid employee involvement in homeland security issues on work time.

World-Class Organization

- Senior leaders empower employees to form homeland security teams within their departments and recognize individual employees for innovative homeland security ideas.
- Senior leaders have formed "study circles" throughout the organization where concerned employees identify disaster-related issues and seek resolution from management.

✔ Approach   ✔ Deployment   ✔ Learning   ✔ Integration

1.1a(2) Senior leaders create an environment for empowerment, innovation, and organizational agility among employees regarding homeland security issues throughout the organization.

+ Strengths

1.
2.
3.

– Opportunities for Improvement

1.
2.
3.

Homeland Security Planning Issues:

Short Term (1 to 2 years)

1.
2.

Long Term (2 years or more)

1.
2.

1.1b How does your organization address management accountability, fiscal accountability, independent internal/external audits, and protection of stockholder/stakeholder interests regarding the organization's homeland security efforts?

Interview notes:

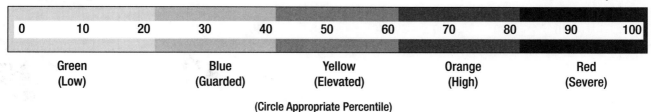

Zero-Based Preparation   **World-Class Preparation**

| 0 | 10 | 20 | 30 | 40 | 50 | 60 | 70 | 80 | 90 | 100 |

| Green (Low) | Blue (Guarded) | Yellow (Elevated) | Orange (High) | Red (Severe) |

(Circle Appropriate Percentile)

Zero-Based Organization

- Organization has no interest in ensuring that homeland security audits are conducted to ensure a safe environment for employees, customers, and suppliers.
- Organization does not associate the identification of homeland security issues and vulnerabilities as a protective initiative for stockholders and stakeholders.

World-Class Organization

- Organization rewards managers and supervisors who have disaster recovery plans documented and in place within their areas of responsibility.
- Organization conducts annual corporate homeland security self-assessments and hires an external security agency to validate assessment findings.

☑ **Approach**   ☑ **Deployment**   ☑ **Learning**   ☑ **Integration**

1.1b Organization addresses management accountability, fiscal accountability, independent internal/external audits, and protection of stockholder/stakeholder interests regarding the organization's homeland security efforts.

+ Strengths

1.

2.

3.

– Opportunities for Improvement

1.

2.

3.

Homeland Security Planning Issues:

Short Term (1 to 2 years)

1.

2.

Long Term (2 years or more)

1.

2.

1.1c(1) How do your senior leaders review and assess the organization's homeland security readiness and capabilities?

Interview notes:

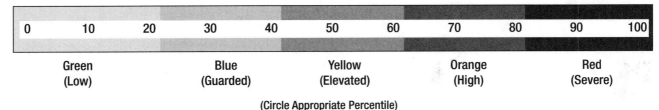

Zero-Based Preparation   **World-Class Preparation**

| 0 | 10 | 20 | 30 | 40 | 50 | 60 | 70 | 80 | 90 | 100 |

| Green | Blue | Yellow | Orange | Red |
| (Low) | (Guarded) | (Elevated) | (High) | (Severe) |

(Circle Appropriate Percentile)

Zero-Based Organization

- Senior leaders do not review and assess the organization's homeland security readiness and capabilities.
- Senior leaders conduct a partial review and assessment of the organization's homeland security readiness and capabilities in order to conduct business with some government contractors.

World-Class Organization

- Senior leaders hold all employees accountable for reviewing and for identifying homeland security issues and vulnerabilities within their work areas. Senior staff meet with employees annually to develop a homeland security readiness plan for their departments.
- Senior leaders review and assess the organization's homeland security plan on a monthly basis.

☑ **Approach**   ☑ **Deployment**   ☑ **Learning**   ☑ **Integration**

1.1c(1) Senior leaders review and assess organization's homeland security readiness and capabilities.

+ Strengths
1.
2.
3.

– Opportunities for Improvement
1.
2.
3.

Homeland Security Planning Issues:

Short Term (1 to 2 years)
1.
2.

Long Term (2 years or more)
1.
2.

1.1c(2) What key homeland security performance measures are regularly reviewed by senior leaders?

Interview notes:

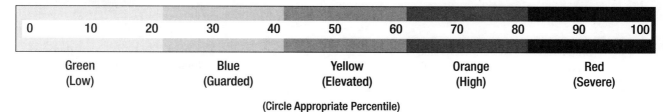

Zero-Based Preparation   **World-Class Preparation**

| 0 | 10 | 20 | 30 | 40 | 50 | 60 | 70 | 80 | 90 | 100 |

| Green
(Low) | Blue
(Guarded) | Yellow
(Elevated) | Orange
(High) | Red
(Severe) |

(Circle Appropriate Percentile)

Zero-Based Organization	**World-Class Organization**
• Senior leaders have not identified key homeland security performance measures to review in case of an organization-wide disaster. • Senior leaders have identified five key homeland security performance measures but conduct random reviews on an inconsistent basis.	• Senior leaders review on a monthly basis their emergency response cycle time, surveillance technology, high-speed Internet access, fax capability, bioterrorism readiness, and worker safety preparation time. • Senior leaders review quarterly radiological attack response time, monitoring of radioactive fallout, evacuation, and decontamination of facilities.

☑ Approach   ☑ Deployment   ☑ Learning   ☑ Integration

1.1c(2) Key homeland security performance measures are regularly reviewed by senior leaders.

+ Strengths

1.

2.

3.

– Opportunities for Improvement

1.

2.

3.

Homeland Security Planning Issues:

Short Term (1 to 2 years)

1.

2.

Long Term (2 years or more)

1.

2.

1.1c(3) How do your senior leaders translate homeland security performance review findings into priorities for continuous and breakthrough improvement that are aligned throughout the organization?

Interview notes:

Zero-Based Preparation   **World-Class Preparation**

| 0 | 10 | 20 | 30 | 40 | 50 | 60 | 70 | 80 | 90 | 100 |

| Green | Blue | Yellow | Orange | Red |
| (Low) | (Guarded) | (Elevated) | (High) | (Severe) |

(Circle Appropriate Percentile)

Zero-Based Organization

- Senior leaders do not translate homeland security performance review findings into priorities that align with and help drive the organization's strategic plans and goals.
- Senior leaders do not consider that homeland security performance review findings can provide a reliable means to guide both improvement and opportunities for innovation that are tied to the organization's key objectives, success factors, and measures.

World-Class Organization

- Senior leaders have translated their homeland security performance review findings for bioterrorism readiness and emergency response cycle time into an action agenda specific for deployment throughout the organization to employees, suppliers, partners, and customers.
- Senior leaders ensure that homeland security performance review findings are aligned with the organization's strategic goals and plans.

☑ **Approach**   ☑ **Deployment**   ☑ **Learning**   ☑ **Integration**

1.1c(3) Senior leaders translate homeland security review findings into priorities for continuous and breakthrough improvement that are aligned throughout the organization.

+ Strengths

1.

2.

3.

– Opportunities for Improvement

1.

2.

3.

Homeland Security Planning Issues:

Short Term (1 to 2 years)

1.

2.

Long Term (2 years or more)

1.

2.

1.1c(4) How does your organization evaluate senior leaders' involvement in homeland security and their performance in securing a safe work environment for all employees?

Interview notes:

Zero-Based Preparation   **World-Class Preparation**

| 0 | 10 | 20 | 30 | 40 | 50 | 60 | 70 | 80 | 90 | 100 |

| Green
(Low) | Blue
(Guarded) | Yellow
(Elevated) | Orange
(High) | Red
(Severe) |

(Circle Appropriate Percentile)

Zero-Based Organization

- Senior leaders' involvement with homeland security issues is not evaluated by employees, suppliers, partners, or customers.

- Senior leaders' involvement in homeland security issues within the organization is evaluated, but results are neither shared nor used for leadership improvement.

World-Class Organization

- Senior leaders' performance is evaluated by employees on an annual basis regarding their involvement in homeland security throughout the organization. Evaluation results are used by senior leaders to improve their performance and involvement.

- Employees, customers, partners, and suppliers focus groups are held semiannually to review senior leadership involvement with homeland security.

☑ Approach ☑ Deployment ☑ Learning ☑ Integration

1.1c(4) Senior leaders are evaluated regarding their involvement in homeland security and their performance in securing a safe work environment for all employees.

+ Strengths

1.

2.

3.

– Opportunities for Improvement

1.

2.

3.

Homeland Security Planning Issues:

Short Term (1 to 2 years)

1.

2.

Long Term (2 years or more)

1.

2.

1.2 Social Responsibility (50 pts.)

Describe how your organization addresses its responsibilities to the public, ensures ethical behavior, and practices good citizenship.

Process

AREAS TO ADDRESS

a. Responsibilities to the Public

(1) How do you address the impacts on society of your products, services, and operations? What are your key compliance processes, measures, and goals for achieving and surpassing regulatory and legal requirements, as appropriate? What are your key processes, measures, and goals for addressing risks associated with your products, services, and operations?

(2) How do you anticipate public concerns with current and future products, services, and operations? How do you prepare for these concerns in a proactive manner?

b. Ethical Behavior

How do you ensure ethical behavior in all stakeholder transactions and interactions? What are your key processes and measures or indicators for monitoring ethical behavior throughout your organization, with key partners, and in your governance structure?

c. Support of Key Communities

How does your organization actively support and strengthen your key communities? How do you identify key communities and determine areas of emphasis for organizational involvement and support? What are your key communities? How do your senior leaders and your employees contribute to improving these communities?

1.2 Percent
Score

 Approach   Deployment   Learning   ✔ Integration

1.2a(1) How does your organization address societal impacts of homeland security on your products, services, and operations?

Interview notes:

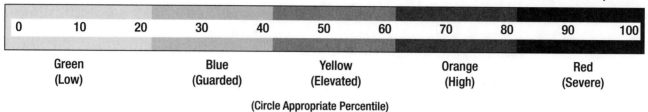

Zero-Based Preparation   **World-Class Preparation**

| 0 | 10 | 20 | 30 | 40 | 50 | 60 | 70 | 80 | 90 | 100 |

Green
(Low)

Blue
(Guarded)

Yellow
(Elevated)

Orange
(High)

Red
(Severe)

(Circle Appropriate Percentile)

Zero-Based Organization

- Organization does not address societal impacts of homeland security on its products, services, and operations and considers it a breach of security to expose its plans to guard against terrorist attacks.
- Organization does not address or detail societal impacts of homeland security on its products, services, and operations.

World-Class Organization

- Organization developed a brochure describing impacts of homeland security against terrorist attacks on its products, services, and operations and distributes the brochure to community agencies, key suppliers, partners, and customers.
- Organization holds public forums with communities where business is conducted to address societal impacts of homeland security on products, services, and operations.

☑ Approach   ☑ Deployment   ☑ Learning   ☑ Integration

1.2a(1) Organization addresses societal impacts of homeland security on products, services, and operations.

+ Strengths
1.
2.
3.

– Opportunities for Improvement
1.
2.
3.

Homeland Security Planning Issues:

Short Term (1 to 2 years)
1.
2.

Long Term (2 years or more)
1.
2.

1.2a(2) How does your organization anticipate the public's homeland security concerns with current and future products, services, and operations?

Interview notes:

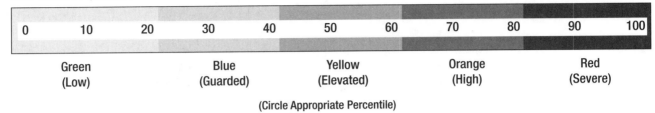

<table>
<tr><td>Zero-Based Preparation</td><td></td><td></td><td></td><td></td><td></td><td>World-Class Preparation</td></tr>
</table>

Zero-Based Organization

- Organization has limited concern for anticipating the public's homeland security concerns with current and future products, services, and operations.
- Organization does not address or hold public forums to gauge homeland security concerns with current and future products, services, and operations.

World-Class Organization

- Organization surveys the public to identify homeland security concerns with current and future products, services, and operations.
- Organization uses its website and 24-hour response telephone system to allow the public to log in and register homeland security concerns with current and future products, services, and operations.

☑ **Approach** ☑ **Deployment** ☑ **Learning** ☑ **Integration**

1.2a(2) Organization anticipates homeland security concerns of the public with current and future products, services, and operations.

+ Strengths

1.

2.

3.

– Opportunities for Improvement

1.

2.

3.

Homeland Security Planning Issues:

Short Term (1 to 2 years)

1.

2.

Long Term (2 years or more)

1.

2.

1.2b How does your organization ensure ethical behavior regarding homeland security issues in all stakeholder transactions and interactions?

Interview notes:

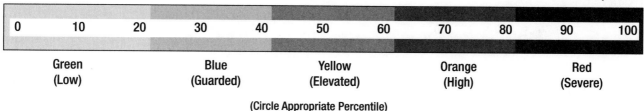

Zero-Based Preparation   **World-Class Preparation**

| 0 | 10 | 20 | 30 | 40 | 50 | 60 | 70 | 80 | 90 | 100 |

| Green
(Low) | | Blue
(Guarded) | | Yellow
(Elevated) | | Orange
(High) | | Red
(Severe) | |

(Circle Appropriate Percentile)

Zero-Based Organization

- Organization does not consider homeland security issues in stakeholder transactions and interactions.
- Organization has no processes in place to ensure ethical behavior in all customer, partner, and supplier transactions.

World-Class Organization

- Organization has developed a code of ethical conduct regarding homeland security issues that impacts products, services, and operations. This statement is distributed to all employees, suppliers, partners, and customers.
- Organization identifies and addresses all ethical key and critical homeland security issues that affect stakeholder transactions and interactions.

☑ Approach   ☑ Deployment   ☑ Learning   ☑ Integration

1.2b Organization ensures ethical behavior regarding homeland security issues in all stakeholder transactions and interactions.

+ Strengths

1.
2.
3.

– Opportunities for Improvement

1.
2.
3.

Homeland Security Planning Issues:

Short Term (1 to 2 years)

1.
2.

Long Term (2 years or more)

1.
2.

1.2c How does your organization support and strengthen homeland security in communities in which business is conducted?

Interview notes:

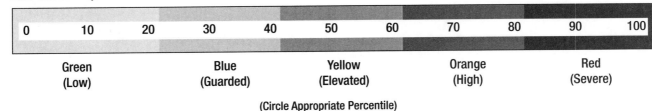

<table>
<tr><td>0</td><td>10</td><td>20</td><td>30</td><td>40</td><td>50</td><td>60</td><td>70</td><td>80</td><td>90</td><td>100</td></tr>
</table>

| Green (Low) | Blue (Guarded) | Yellow (Elevated) | Orange (High) | Red (Severe) |

(Circle Appropriate Percentile)

Zero-Based Organization

- Organization does not contribute money or employee volunteers for homeland security initiatives within the communities in which business is conducted.
- Organization offers no community involvement regarding homeland security.

World-Class Organization

- Organization recognizes employees who promote homeland security issues in local, state, national, and industry organizations.
- Organization provides extra pay incentives for employees who volunteer their time to serve in community response teams within communities where business is conducted.

[✔] Approach   [✔] Deployment   [✔] Learning   [✔] Integration

1.2c Organization supports and strengthens homeland security in communities in which business is conducted.

+ Strengths

1.

2.

3.

– Opportunities for Improvement

1.

2.

3.

Homeland Security Planning Issues:

Short Term (1 to 2 years)

1.

2.

Long Term (2 years or more)

1.

2.

Notes

4
Category 2
Strategic Planning

2 Strategic Planning (85 pts.)[11]

The Strategic Planning Category examines how your organization develops strategic objectives and action plans for homeland security. Also examined are how your chosen strategic objectives and action plans for homeland security are deployed and how progress is measured.

 Forms can be downloaded from the CD-ROM located inside the back cover of this book.

2.1 Strategy Development (40 pts.)

Process

Describe how your organization establishes its strategic objectives, including how it enhances its competitive position, overall performance, and future success.

AREAS TO ADDRESS

a. **Strategy Development Process**

(1) What is your overall strategic planning process? What are the key steps? Who are the key participants? What are your short- and longer-term planning time horizons? How are these time horizons set? How does your strategic planning process address these time horizons?

(2) How do you ensure that strategic planning addresses the key factors listed below? How do you collect and analyze relevant data and information to address these factors as they relate to your strategic planning?

- Your customer and market needs, expectations, and opportunities
- Your competitive environment and your capabilities relative to competitors
- Technological and other key innovations or changes that might affect your products and services and how you operate
- Your strengths and weaknesses including human and other resources
- Your opportunities to redirect resources to higher priority products, services, or areas
- Financial, societal and ethical, regulatory, and other potential risks
- Changes in the national or global economy
- Factors unique to your organization, including partner and supply chain needs, strengths, and weaknesses

b. **Strategic Objectives**

(1) What are your key strategic objectives and your timetable for accomplishing them? What are your most important goals for these strategic objectives ?

(2) How do your strategic objectives address the challenges identified in your Organizational Profile? How do you ensure that your strategic objectives balance short- and longer-term challenges and opportunities? How do you ensure that your strategic objectives balance the needs of all key stakeholders?

2.1 Percent
Score

 Approach Deployment ✔ Learning Integration

2.1a(1) What is your organization's overall strategic planning process for homeland security?

Interview notes:

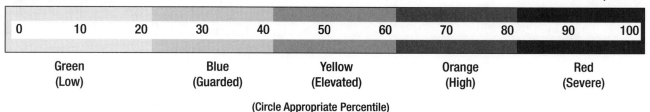

Zero-Based Preparation   **World-Class Preparation**

| 0 | 10 | 20 | 30 | 40 | 50 | 60 | 70 | 80 | 90 | 100 |

| Green | Blue | Yellow | Orange | Red |
| (Low) | (Guarded) | (Elevated) | (High) | (Severe) |

(Circle Appropriate Percentile)

Zero-Based Organization

- Organization does not have an overall strategic planning process in place for homeland security.
- Organization has not developed a vision and identified strategic objectives to implement a plan for homeland security issues.

World-Class Organization

- Organization has each division identify and develop short- and longer-term objectives for homeland security. All division plans are merged into an organization-wide plan for homeland security.
- Organization involves input from all employee levels when developing an overall strategic planning process for homeland security.

☑ Approach   ☑ Deployment   ☑ Learning   ☑ Integration

2.1a(1) Organization's overall homeland security strategic planning process.

+ Strengths

1.

2.

3.

– Opportunities for Improvement

1.

2.

3.

Homeland Security Planning Issues:

Short Term (1 to 2 years)

1.

2.

Long Term (2 years or more)

1.

2.

2.1a(2)   How does your organization ensure that strategic planning addresses key homeland security factors (e.g., customer/market needs, competitive environment, technology needs, human resources, redirecting resources, financial risks, societal risks, national/global economy changes, partner/supply chain needs)?

Interview notes:

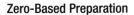

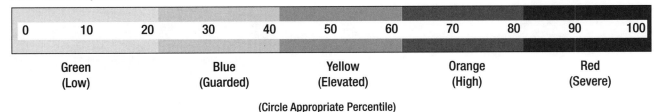

Zero-Based Preparation   World-Class Preparation

| 0 | 10 | 20 | 30 | 40 | 50 | 60 | 70 | 80 | 90 | 100 |

Green (Low)   Blue (Guarded)   Yellow (Elevated)   Orange (High)   Red (Severe)

(Circle Appropriate Percentile)

Zero-Based Organization

- Organization has not considered key homeland security factors in its strategic plan such as a disruption of its corporate intranet system and disruption of transportation for shipping and receiving goods and services from various supply chain needs.

- Organization has not identified key homeland security factors to develop a planning approach that will ensure continuity within its operations in case of a major business disruption.

World-Class Organization

- Organization has a strategic plan to manage homeland security issues and to mitigate future security risks for the organization.

- Organization's strategic plan for homeland security addresses increased technology needs, identification of product, service, and operational risks, and redirection of financial and human resources.

☑ Approach   ☑ Deployment   ☑ Learning   ☑ Integration

2.1a(2)   Organization addresses key homeland security factors in its strategic plan.

+ Strengths

1.

2.

3.

– Opportunities for Improvement

1.

2.

3.

Homeland Security Planning Issues:

Short Term (1 to 2 years)

1.

2.

Long Term (2 years or more)

1.

2.

2.1b(1) What are your organization's key strategic objectives for homeland security and your timetable for accomplishing them?

Interview notes:

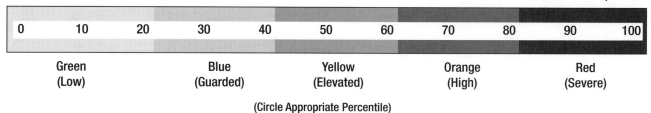

Zero-Based Preparation   **World-Class Preparation**

| 0 | 10 | 20 | 30 | 40 | 50 | 60 | 70 | 80 | 90 | 100 |

Green (Low)   Blue (Guarded)   Yellow (Elevated)   Orange (High)   Red (Severe)

(Circle Appropriate Percentile)

Zero-Based Organization

- Organization has not identified key strategic objectives for homeland security.
- Organization is relying on local community, state, and federal agencies for protection from homeland security threats and attacks.

World-Class Organization

- Organization's key strategic objectives for homeland security is to protect its critical infrastructure, which includes the development of a corporate preparedness plan that includes protection of the IT network, transportation, and laboratories throughout the organization.
- Organization has prepared a timetable for accomplishing a corporate preparedness plan for homeland security.

☑ Approach ☑ Deployment ☑ Learning ☑ Integration

2.1b(1) Organization's key strategic objectives for homeland security and timetable for accomplishing them.

+ Strengths

1.
2.
3.

– Opportunities for Improvement

1.
2.
3.

Homeland Security Planning Issues:

Short Term (1 to 2 years)

1.
2.

Long Term (2 years or more)

1.
2.

2.1b(2) How does your organization ensure that strategic objectives for homeland security address challenges and opportunities and balance the needs of all key stakeholders?

Interview notes:

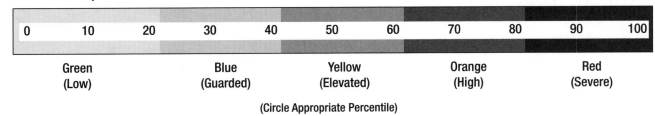

Zero-Based Preparation   **World-Class Preparation**

| 0 | 10 | 20 | 30 | 40 | 50 | 60 | 70 | 80 | 90 | 100 |

Green (Low)   Blue (Guarded)   Yellow (Elevated)   Orange (High)   Red (Severe)

(Circle Appropriate Percentile)

Zero-Based Organization

- Organization does not align strategic objectives for homeland security with its short- and long-term business plans and goals and ensure that key stakeholders' homeland security needs are addressed.
- Organization does not focus on specific security challenges and stakeholder needs when identifying and developing strategic objectives for homeland security.

World-Class Organization

- Organization ensures that its strategic objectives for homeland security balance the needs of all employees, key suppliers, partners, and customers.
- Organization addresses strategic homeland security objectives that are most important to continuation of business success and overall business operations.

☑ Approach   ☑ Deployment   ☑ Learning   ☑ Integration

2.1b(2) Organization's strategic objectives for homeland security address challenges and opportunities and balance all key stakeholder needs.

+ Strengths

1.

2.

3.

– Opportunities for Improvement

1.

2.

3.

Homeland Security Planning Issues:

Short Term (1 to 2 years)

1.

2.

Long Term (2 years or more)

1.

2.

2.2 Strategy Deployment (45 pts.)

Process

Describe how your organization converts its strategic objectives into action plans. Summarize your organization's action plans and related key performance measures or indicators. Project your organization's future performance on these key performance measures or indicators.

AREAS TO ADDRESS

a. Strategy Development and Deployment

(1) How do you develop and deploy action plans to achieve your key strategic objectives? How do you allocate resources to ensure accomplishment of your action plans? How do you ensure that the key changes resulting from actions plans can be sustained?

(2) What are your key short- and longer-term action plans? What are the key changes, if any, in your products and services, your customers and markets, and your way of operating?

(3) What are your key human resource plans that derive from your short- and longer-term strategic objectives and action plans?

(4) What are your key performance measures or indicators for tracking progress on your action plans? How do you ensure that your overall action plan measurement system reinforces organizational alignment? How do you ensure that the measurement system covers all key deployment areas and stakeholders?

b. Performance Projection

For the key performance measures or indicators identified in 2.2a(4), what are your performance projections for both your short- and longer-term planning time horizons? How does your projected performance compare with competitors' projected performance? How does it compare with key benchmarks, goals, and past performance, as appropriate?

2.2 Percent Score

☑ **Approach**   ☑ **Deployment**   ☑ **Learning**   ☑ **Integration**

2.2a(1) How does your organization develop and deploy action plans to achieve your key homeland security strategic objectives?

Interview notes:

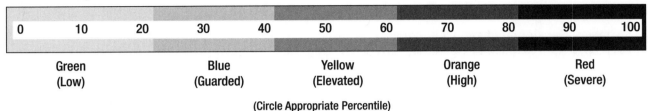

Zero-Based Preparation   World-Class Preparation

| 0 | 10 | 20 | 30 | 40 | 50 | 60 | 70 | 80 | 90 | 100 |

Green
(Low)

Blue
(Guarded)

Yellow
(Elevated)

Orange
(High)

Red
(Severe)

(Circle Appropriate Percentile)

Zero-Based Organization

- Organization does not provide either financial or human resources to develop and deploy action plans to achieve homeland security goals and objectives.
- Organization has developed homeland security action plans but does not gauge progress toward meeting these goals.

World-Class Organization

- Organization's senior leadership sets and communicates homeland security goals and directions to all employee levels.
- Organization provides financial and human resources to develop and deploy action plans to achieve key homeland security strategic objectives.

✔ Approach   ✔ Deployment   ✔ Learning   ✔ Integration

2.2a(1) Organization develops and deploys action plans to achieve key homeland security strategic objectives.

+ Strengths

1.

2.

3.

– Opportunities for Improvement

1.

2.

3.

Homeland Security Planning Issues:

Short Term (1 to 2 years)

1.

2.

Long Term (2 years or more)

1.

2.

2.2a(2) What are your organization's key short-and longer-term action plans for homeland security?

Interview notes:

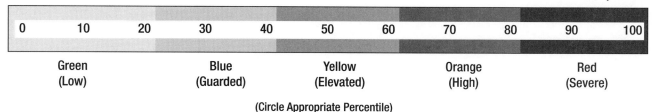

Zero-Based Preparation   **World-Class Preparation**

| 0 | 10 | 20 | 30 | 40 | 50 | 60 | 70 | 80 | 90 | 100 |

| Green | Blue | Yellow | Orange | Red |
| (Low) | (Guarded) | (Elevated) | (High) | (Severe) |

(Circle Appropriate Percentile)

Zero-Based Organization

- Organization has no action plans developed for homeland security.
- Organization collects anecdotal information regarding exposure to a terrorist attack on its organizational infrastructure. Limited action plans are developed for homeland security.

World-Class Organization

- Organization's key short- and longer-term action plans for homeland security include an emergency management plan, hazardous materials training for all employees, and an organization assessment of potential threat areas.
- Organization has conducted a terrorist risk assessment and developed short- and long-term action plans that address a potential threat.

✔ **Approach**   ✔ **Deployment**   ✔ **Learning**   ✔ **Integration**

2.2a(2) Organization's key short- and longer-term action plans for homeland security.

+ Strengths

1.

2.

3.

– Opportunities for Improvement

1.

2.

3.

Homeland Security Planning Issues:

Short Term (1 to 2 years)

1.

2.

Long Term (2 years or more)

1.

2.

2.2a(3) What are your organization's key human resource plans that derive from short- and longer-term homeland security strategic objectives and action plans?

Interview notes:

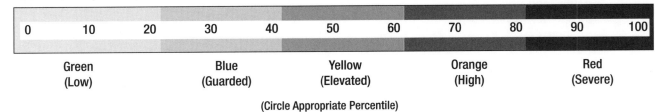

Zero-Based Preparation					World-Class Preparation

0	10	20	30	40	50	60	70	80	90	100

Green (Low)	Blue (Guarded)	Yellow (Elevated)	Orange (High)	Red (Severe)

(Circle Appropriate Percentile)

Zero-Based Organization

- Organization does not have a human resource plan that addresses homeland security issues.
- Organization has not aligned its homeland security goals and objectives with its human resource plan.

World-Class Organization

- Organization has developed a human resource plan for homeland security that is aligned with short- and long-term strategic plans and goals.
- Organization involves cross-functional employee teams to develop a homeland security human resource plan. The plan is aligned with the organization's strategic goals and objectives.

☑ Approach   ☑ Deployment   ☑ Learning   ☑ Integration

2.2a(3) Organization's key human resource plans that derive from short- and longer-term homeland security strategic objectives and action plans.

+ Strengths

1.
2.
3.

– Opportunities for Improvement

1.
2.
3.

Homeland Security Planning Issues:

Short Term (1 to 2 years)

1.
2.

Long Term (2 years or more)

1.
2.

2.2a(4) What are your organization's key performance measures or indicators for tracking progress on homeland security action plans?

Interview notes:

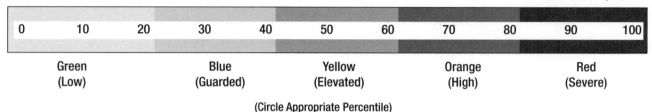

Green
(Low)
Blue
(Guarded)
Yellow
(Elevated)
Orange
(High)
Red
(Severe)

(Circle Appropriate Percentile)

Zero-Based Organization

- Organization does not track progress on its homeland security action plans.
- Organization has no performance measures in place to gauge homeland security action plan progress.

World-Class Organization

- Organization has identified a set of performance measures to track its homeland security action plans.
- Organization has conducted a homeland security risk assessment and identified three indicators to track progress regarding action plans. These include cycle time, completion date of action plans, and impact on the organization.

☑ Approach   ☑ Deployment   ☑ Learning   ☑ Integration

2.2a(4) Organization's key performance measures or indicators for tracking progress on homeland security action plans.

+ Strengths

1.

2.

3.

– Opportunities for Improvement

1.

2.

3.

Homeland Security Planning Issues:

Short Term (1 to 2 years)

1.

2.

Long Term (2 years or more)

1.

2.

2.2b How are your organization's performance projections used to track homeland security progress?

Interview notes:

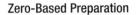

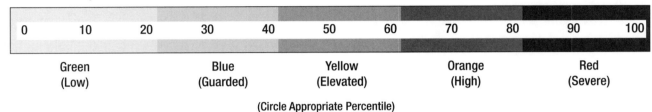

| Zero-Based Preparation | | | | | | | | | | World-Class Preparation |

0   10   20   30   40   50   60   70   80   90   100

Green
(Low)

Blue
(Guarded)

Yellow
(Elevated)

Orange
(High)

Red
(Severe)

(Circle Appropriate Percentile)

Zero-Based Organization

- Organization does not use performance projections to gauge homeland security progress.
- Organization uses no performance projections or indicators and does not compare its homeland security performance against key benchmark goals and past performance.

World-Class Organization

- Organization's performance projections are used to improve its rate of improvement for homeland security issues and serve as a key diagnostic management tool.
- Organization uses performance projections to gauge new and innovative homeland security systems.

☑ Approach   ☑ Deployment   ☑ Learning   ☑ Integration

2.2b Organization's performance projections used in tracking homeland security progress.

+ Strengths
1.
2.
3.

– Opportunities for Improvement
1.
2.
3.

Homeland Security Planning Issues:

Short Term (1 to 2 years)
1.
2.

Long Term (2 years or more)
1.
2.

Notes

5

Category 3
Customer and Market Focus

3 Customer and Market Focus (85 pts.)[12]

The Customer and Market Focus Category examines how your organization determines requirements, expectations, and preferences of customers and markets for the organization's homeland security initiatives. Also examined is how your organization builds relationships with customers and determines the key factors that lead to customer acquisition, satisfaction, loyalty, retention, and to business expansion regarding homeland security initiatives and issues.

 Forms can be downloaded from the CD-ROM located inside the back cover of this book.

3.1 Customer and Market Knowledge (40 pts.)

Describe how your organization determines requirements, expectations, and preferences of customers and markets to ensure the continuing relevance of your products and services and to develop new opportunities.

AREAS TO ADDRESS

a. **Customer and Market Knowledge**

(1) How do you determine or target customers, customer groups, and market segments? How do you include customers of competitors and other potential customers and markets in this determination?

(2) How do you listen and learn to determine key customer requirements and expectations (including product and service features) and their relative importance to customers' purchasing decisions? How do determination methods vary for different customers or customer groups? How do you use relevant information from current and former customers, including marketing and sales information, customer loyalty and retention data, win/lose analysis, and complaints? How do you use this information for purposes of product and service planning, marketing, process improvements, and other business development?

(3) How do you keep your listening and learning methods current with business needs and directions?

3.1 Percent
Score

☑ Approach   ☑ Deployment   ☑ Learning   ☑ Integration

3.1a(1) How does your organization determine or target customers, customer groups, and market segments for homeland security initiatives?

Interview notes:

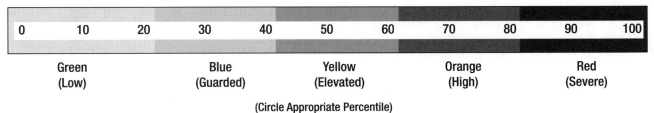

Zero-Based Preparation   **World-Class Preparation**

| 0 | 10 | 20 | 30 | 40 | 50 | 60 | 70 | 80 | 90 | 100 |

Green
(Low)

Blue
(Guarded)

Yellow
(Elevated)

Orange
(High)

Red
(Severe)

(Circle Appropriate Percentile)

Zero-Based Organization

- Organization does not segment or survey customers and customer groups regarding their homeland security needs and expectations.
- Organization has no concern for segmenting customers regarding homeland security initiatives. All customers are treated the same regarding security precautions.

World-Class Organization

- Organization segments customer groups and market segments to determine and target its application of homeland security initiatives.
- Organization surveys customers and customer groups, aggregates the data, and determines level of security risk based on results.

☑ Approach   ☑ Deployment   ☑ Learning   ☑ Integration

3.1a(1) Organization determines and targets customers, customer groups, and market segments for homeland security initiatives.

+ Strengths

1.

2.

3.

– Opportunities for Improvement

1.

2.

3.

Homeland Security Planning Issues:

Short Term (1 to 2 years)

1.

2.

Long Term (2 years or more)

1.

2.

3.1a(2) How does your organization listen and learn to determine key customer requirements and expectations regarding homeland security issues?

Interview notes:

Zero-Based Preparation   **World-Class Preparation**

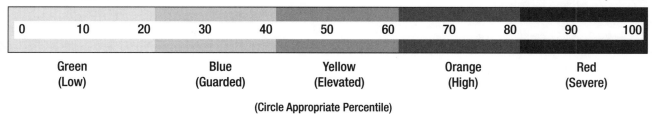

(Circle Appropriate Percentile)

Zero-Based Organization

- Organization does not address homeland security requirements and expectations with its customers.
- Organization has identified a limited number of key customers to interview concerning their requirements and expectations regarding homeland security issues. The results of these interviews determine what homeland security issues will be deployed to all customers.

World-Class Organization

- Organization's customer-contact employees meet monthly with key customers to determine their requirements and expectations regarding homeland security issues.
- Organization conducts annual surveys and holds quarterly focus groups with key customers to determine their homeland security requirements and expectations.

☑ **Approach**   ☑ **Deployment**   ☑ **Learning**   ☑ **Integration**

3.1a(2) Organization listens and learns to determine key customer requirements and expectations regarding homeland security issues.

+ Strengths

1.
2.
3.

– Opportunities for Improvement

1.
2.
3.

Homeland Security Planning Issues:

Short Term (1 to 2 years)

1.
2.

Long Term (2 years or more)

1.
2.

3.1a(3) How does your organization keep listening and learning methods current with homeland security needs and directions?

Interview notes:

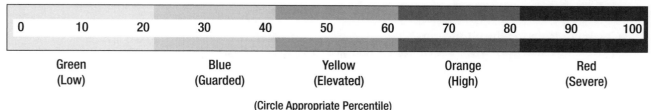

Zero-Based Preparation   World-Class Preparation

| 0 | 10 | 20 | 30 | 40 | 50 | 60 | 70 | 80 | 90 | 100 |

| Green (Low) | Blue (Guarded) | Yellow (Elevated) | Orange (High) | Red (Severe) |

(Circle Appropriate Percentile)

Zero-Based Organization

- Organization is not concerned with using listening posts to better understand customer concerns and expectations regarding homeland security issues. The organization has no concern for changing and incorporating current methods.
- Organization seldom changes its methods for gauging homeland security needs and directions.

World-Class Organization

- Organization annually surveys international, federal, state, and local agencies to ensure that homeland security listening and learning methods for its customers are current with global standards.
- Organization hosts annual focus groups of homeland security subject-matter experts to ensure that its listening and learning methods are current and state of the art.

☑ Approach   ☑ Deployment   ☑ Learning   ☑ Integration

3.1a(3) Organization keeps listening and learning methods current with homeland security needs and directions.

+ Strengths

1.

2.

3.

– Opportunities for Improvement

1.

2.

3.

Homeland Security Planning Issues:

Short Term (1 to 2 years)

1.

2.

Long Term (2 years or more)

1.

2.

3.2 Customer Relationships and Satisfaction (45 pts.)

Describe how your organization determines and builds relationships to acquire, satisfy, and retain customers; to increase customer loyalty; and to develop new opportunities. Describe also how your organization determines customer satisfaction.

AREAS TO ADDRESS

a. Customer Relationship Building

(1) How do you build relationships to acquire customers, to meet and exceed their expectations, to increase loyalty and repeat business, and to gain positive referrals?

(2) What are your key access mechanisms for customers to seek information, conduct business, and make complaints? How do you determine key customer contact requirements for each mode of customer access? How do you ensure that these contact requirements are deployed to all people and processes involved in the customer response chain?

(3) What is your complaint-management process? How do you ensure that complaints are resolved effectively and promptly? How are complaints aggregated and analyzed for use in improvement throughout your organization and by your partners?

(4) How do you keep your approaches to building relationships and providing customer access current with business needs and directions?

b. Customer Satisfaction Determination

(1) How do you determine customer satisfaction and dissatisfaction? How do these determination methods differ among customer groups? How do you ensure that your measurements capture actionable information for use in exceeding your customers' expectations, securing their future business, and gaining positive referrals? How do you use customer satisfaction and dissatisfaction information for improvement?

(2) How do you follow up with customers on products, services, and transaction quality to receive prompt and actionable feedback?

(3) How do you obtain and use information on your customers' satisfaction relative to customers' satisfaction with your competitors and/or industry benchmarks?

(4) How do you keep your approaches to determining satisfaction current with business needs and directions?

3.2 Percent
Score

 Approach   Deployment   Learning   Integration

3.2a(1) How does your organization build relationships with customers regarding homeland security issues?

Interview notes:

Zero-Based Preparation   **World-Class Preparation**

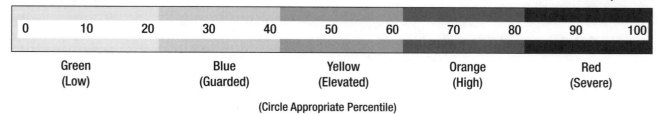

| Green
(Low) | Blue
(Guarded) | Yellow
(Elevated) | Orange
(High) | Red
(Severe) |

(Circle Appropriate Percentile)

Zero-Based Organization

- Organization's senior staff are the only ones involved with customers to build relationships regarding homeland security issues.
- Organization does not systematically identify and determine customer needs and expectations regarding homeland security issues and use findings to maintain and build ongoing relationships.

World-Class Organization

- Organization holds semiannual roundtable discussions with key customers and includes state and local security agencies, legislators, and city council members to build better customer relationships regarding homeland security issues.
- Organization conducts an annual community partnership forum for key customers with key government and community leaders to share and communicate the organization's plans and initiatives.

☑ Approach   ☑ Deployment   ☑ Learning   ☑ Integration

3.2a(1) Organization builds relationships with customers regarding homeland security issues.

+ Strengths
1.
2.
3.

– Opportunities for Improvement
1.
2.
3.

Homeland Security Planning Issues:

Short Term (1 to 2 years)
1.
2.

Long Term (2 years or more)
1.
2.

3.2a(2) What are your organization's key access mechanisms for customers to seek homeland security information, conduct business, and make complaints regarding homeland security issues?

Interview notes:

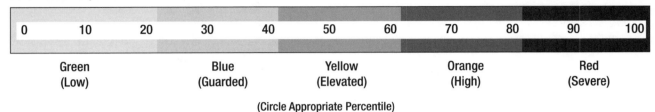

Zero-Based Preparation				World-Class Preparation
0 10 20	30 40	50 60	70 80	90 100
Green (Low)	Blue (Guarded)	Yellow (Elevated)	Orange (High)	Red (Severe)

(Circle Appropriate Percentile)

Zero-Based Organization

- Organization does not have a dedicated 24-hour mechanism in place to address customer's requests, concerns, and complaints regarding homeland security issues.
- Organization does not have a process in place for customers to seek homeland security information, conduct business regarding homeland security issues, and register homeland security complaints.

World-Class Organization

- Organization has a 24-hour, 1-800 phone line and help desk to address homeland security issues and complaints.
- Organization has a customer website devoted to homeland security. The website allows customers to seek information, conduct business, and register complaints regarding homeland security issues and concerns.

☑ Approach   ☑ Deployment   ☑ Learning   ☑ Integration

3.2a(2) Organization has key access mechanisms for customers to seek homeland security information, conduct business, and make complaints regarding homeland security issues.

+ Strengths

1.
2.
3.

– Opportunities for Improvement

1.
2.
3.

Homeland Security Planning Issues:

Short Term (1 to 2 years)

1.
2.

Long Term (2 years or more)

1.
2.

3.2a(3) What is your organization's homeland security complaint-management process?

Interview notes:

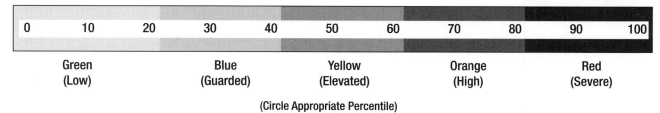

Zero-Based Preparation										World-Class Preparation
0	10	20	30	40	50	60	70	80	90	100

Green	Blue	Yellow	Orange	Red
(Low)	(Guarded)	(Elevated)	(High)	(Severe)

(Circle Appropriate Percentile)

Zero-Based Organization

- Organization has no consistent process in place for customers to register homeland security complaints.
- Organization does not address or register homeland security complaints.

World-Class Organization

- Organization has a documented homeland security resolution process in place that ensures that all complaints are resolved both effectively and promptly.
- Organization has developed a web page on its website for customers to register homeland security complaints 24 hours a day. Response time for all complaints is guaranteed to be within 12 hours.

✔ **Approach**   ✔ **Deployment**   ✔ **Learning**   ✔ **Integration**

3.2a(3) Organization has s homeland security complaint management process.

+ Strengths
1.
2.
3.

– Opportunities for Improvement
1.
2.
3.

Homeland Security Planning Issues:

Short Term (1 to 2 years)
1.
2.

Long Term (2 years or more)
1.
2.

3.2a(4) How does your organization keep approaches to building relationships and providing customer access current with homeland security needs and directions?

Interview notes:

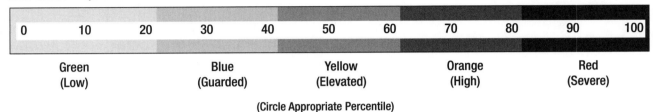

Zero-Based Preparation   **World-Class Preparation**

| 0 | 10 | 20 | 30 | 40 | 50 | 60 | 70 | 80 | 90 | 100 |

Green
(Low)
Blue
(Guarded)
Yellow
(Elevated)
Orange
(High)
Red
(Severe)

(Circle Appropriate Percentile)

Zero-Based Organization

- Organization is not concerned with its approach to building relationships and providing customers access to current homeland security needs and directions.
- Organization does not address relationship management with customers regarding homeland security issues.

World-Class Organization

- Organization conducts formal benchmarks to organizations known to have "best practice" homeland security access and approaches for customers. The organization uses its findings to validate its approaches.
- Organization uses industry focus groups to review and validate its approaches to building relationships and providing customers access to homeland security issues and directions.

☑ **Approach**   ☑ **Deployment**   ☑ **Learning**   ☑ **Integration**

3.2a(4) Organization's approaches to building relationships and providing customer access current with homeland security needs and directions.

+ Strengths

1.

2.

3.

– Opportunities for Improvement

1.

2.

3.

Homeland Security Planning Issues:

Short Term (1 to 2 years)

1.

2.

Long Term (2 years or more)

1.

2.

3.2b(1) How does your organization determine customer satisfaction and dissatisfaction with homeland security initiatives?

Interview notes:

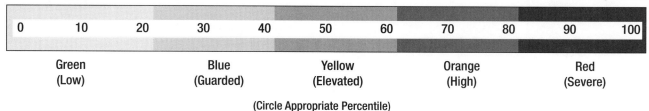

Zero-Based Preparation   **World-Class Preparation**

| 0 | 10 | 20 | 30 | 40 | 50 | 60 | 70 | 80 | 90 | 100 |

Green (Low)   Blue (Guarded)   Yellow (Elevated)   Orange (High)   Red (Severe)

(Circle Appropriate Percentile)

Zero-Based Organization

- Organization has no processes in place to determine customer satisfaction/dissatisfaction with homeland security issues and initiatives.
- Organization collects customer satisfaction/dissatisfaction data regarding homeland security issues but does not aggregate data and use to identify areas for process improvements.

World-Class Organization

- Organization surveys customers annually to determine their satisfaction/dissatisfaction with homeland security initiatives.
- Organization hosts a blue-ribbon customer panel annually to document its overall satisfaction/dissatisfaction with homeland security initiatives. Findings are aggregated by market segments and used for process improvement.

☑ Approach   ☑ Deployment   ☑ Learning   ☑ Integration

3.2b(1) Organization determines customer satisfaction and dissatisfaction with homeland security initiatives.

+ Strengths

1.

2.

3.

– Opportunities for Improvement

1.

2.

3.

Homeland Security Planning Issues:

Short Term (1 to 2 years)

1.

2.

Long Term (2 years or more)

1.

2.

3.2b(2) How does your organization follow up with customers regarding homeland security initiatives that involve products, services, and transactions and ensure that they receive prompt and actionable feedback?

Interview notes:

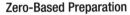

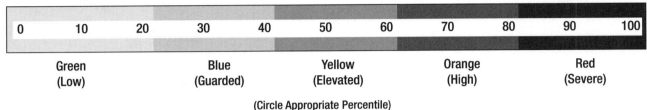

Zero-Based Preparation   **World-Class Preparation**

| 0 | 10 | 20 | 30 | 40 | 50 | 60 | 70 | 80 | 90 | 100 |

Green
(Low)

Blue
(Guarded)

Yellow
(Elevated)

Orange
(High)

Red
(Severe)

(Circle Appropriate Percentile)

Zero-Based Organization

- Organization does not have a documented follow-up procedure for customer complaints regarding homeland security initiatives that involve products, services, and transactions.
- Organization does not consistently follow up on customer complaints regarding homeland security issues and interactions.

World-Class Organization

- Organization follow-up is within two hours after a customer complains about a homeland security issue. An improvement strategy is developed with customer consensus within four hours and a plan is documented and deployed back to the customer within six hours.
- Organization has a two-hour follow-up guarantee on all customer complaints and concerns regarding homeland security initiatives that involve products, services, and transactions.

☑ Approach   ☑ Deployment   ☑ Learning   ☑ Integration

3.2b(2) Organization follows up with customers regarding homeland security initiatives that involve products, services, and transactions.

+ Strengths
1.
2.
3.

– Opportunities for Improvement
1.
2.
3.

Homeland Security Planning Issues:

Short Term (1 to 2 years)
1.
2.

Long Term (2 years or more)
1.
2.

3.2b(3) How does your organization obtain, use, and compare customer satisfaction with your organization's homeland security initiatives relative to your competitors and/or industry benchmarks?

Interview notes:

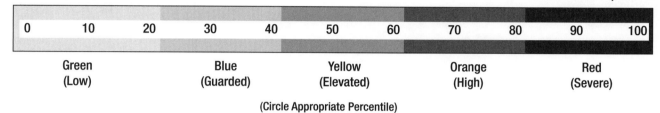

Zero-Based Organization

- Organization does not use comparison and benchmark data to gauge customer satisfaction with the organization's homeland security initiatives.

- Organization's data comparisons regarding customer satisfaction with homeland security initiatives relative to the organization's competition appear anecdotal.

World-Class Organization

- Organization uses benchmark and comparison data to improve its homeland security initiatives with customers.

- Organization uses government, industry, and market homeland security data as a benchmark to gauge overall customer satisfaction with the organization's homeland security initiatives.

☑ Approach   ☑ Deployment   ☑ Learning   ☑ Integration

3.2b(3) Organization's use and comparison of customer satisfaction with homeland security initiatives relative to competitors and/or industry benchmarks.

+ Strengths

1.

2.

3.

– Opportunities for Improvement

1.

2.

3.

Homeland Security Planning Issues:

Short Term (1 to 2 years)

1.

2.

Long Term (2 years or more)

1.

2.

3.2b(4) How does your organization keep approaches to determining customer satisfaction current with homeland security needs and directions?

Interview notes:

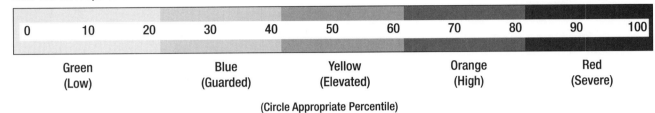

Zero-Based Preparation   **World-Class Preparation**

| 0 | 10 | 20 | 30 | 40 | 50 | 60 | 70 | 80 | 90 | 100 |

| Green | Blue | Yellow | Orange | Red |
| (Low) | (Guarded) | (Elevated) | (High) | (Severe) |

(Circle Appropriate Percentile)

Zero-Based Organization

- Organization has no process in place to determine if customer satisfaction with the organization's approach regarding homeland security issues and initiatives is current and addresses their security needs and directions.

- Organization is not concerned with gauging the currency of its approach to determine customer satisfaction with homeland security needs and directions.

World-Class Organization

- Organization conducts periodic customer surveys to ensure that homeland security initiatives offered to customers are current with their security needs and directions.

- Customer focus groups are conducted biannually to ensure that the organization's approaches for determining customer satisfaction with homeland security needs and directions are current.

☑ Approach   ☑ Deployment   ☑ Learning   ☑ Integration

3.2b(4) Organization's approaches to determining customer satisfaction are kept current with homeland security needs and directions.

+ Strengths

1.
2.
3.

– Opportunities for Improvement

1.
2.
3.

Homeland Security Planning Issues:

Short Term (1 to 2 years)

1.
2.

Long Term (2 years or more)

1.
2.

Notes

6 Category 4
Measurement, Analysis, and Knowledge Management

4 Measurement, Analysis, and Knowledge Management (90 pts.)[13]

The Measurement, Analysis, and Knowledge Management Category examines how your organization selects, gathers, analyzes, manages, and improves its data, information, and knowledge assets for homeland security.

 Forms can be downloaded from the CD-ROM located inside the back cover of this book.

4.1 Measurement and Analysis of Organizational Performance (45 pts.)

Describe how your organization measures, analyzes, aligns, and improves its performance data and information at all levels and in all parts of your organization.

AREAS TO ADDRESS

a. Performance Measurement

(1) How do you select, collect, align, and integrate data and information for tracking daily operations and for tracking overall organizational performance? How do you use these data and this information to support organizational decision making and innovation?

(2) How do you select and ensure the effective use of key comparative data and information to support operational and strategic decision making and innovation?

(3) How do you keep your performance measurement system current with business needs and directions? How do you ensure that your performance measurement system is sensitive to rapid or unexpected organizational or external changes?

b. Performance Analysis

(1) What analyses do you perform to support your senior leaders' organizational performance review? What analyses do you perform to support your organization's strategic planning?

(2) How do you communicate the results of organizational-level analyses to work-group and functional-level operations to enable effective support for their decision making?

4.1 Percent
Score

 Approach   Deployment   Learning   Integration

4.1a(1) How does your organization select, collect, align, and integrate data and information for tracking daily and overall performance of homeland security?

Interview notes:

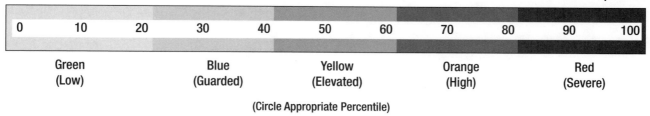

Zero-Based Preparation				World-Class Preparation

| 0 | 10 | 20 | 30 | 40 | 50 | 60 | 70 | 80 | 90 | 100 |

Green (Low)   Blue (Guarded)   Yellow (Elevated)   Orange (High)   Red (Severe)

(Circle Appropriate Percentile)

Zero-Based Organization

- Organization has no formal selection process in place for information and data to support the organization's homeland security processes, strategic action plans, and performance management systems.
- Organization anecdotally selects and uses homeland security information and data to track overall performance of homeland security initiatives.

World-Class Organization

- Organization has a documented process for the selection, collection, alignment, and tracking of the organization's homeland security data and information.
- Organization has all homeland security data and information color-coded by terrorist risk levels, based on the homeland security advisory system (HSAS). Data are tracked by attack risk levels.

☑ Approach   ☑ Deployment   ☑ Learning   ☑ Integration

4.1a(1) Organization selects, collects, aligns, and integrates data and information for tracking daily and overall performance of homeland security initiatives.

+ Strengths
1.
2.
3.

– Opportunities for Improvement
1.
2.
3.

Homeland Security Planning Issues:

Short Term (1 to 2 years)
1.
2.

Long Term (2 years or more)
1.
2.

4.1a(2) How does your organization select and ensure the effective use of key homeland security comparative data and information to support operational and strategic decision making and innovation?

Interview notes:

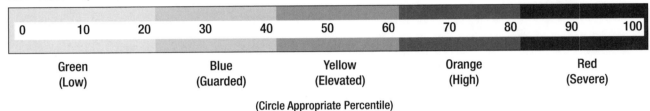

Zero-Based Preparation   **World-Class Preparation**

| 0 | 10 | 20 | 30 | 40 | 50 | 60 | 70 | 80 | 90 | 100 |

Green
(Low)

Blue
(Guarded)

Yellow
(Elevated)

Orange
(High)

Red
(Severe)

(Circle Appropriate Percentile)

Zero-Based Organization

- Organization does not use comparative data and information to support homeland security decision making.
- Organization makes no homeland security comparisons against other organizations known for their best practices.

World-Class Organization

- Organization selects data by reviewing "risk of attack" levels. The selected high-priority data and information are compared against industry and governmental organizations' "best practice" homeland security initiatives and used to support strategic decision making throughout the organization.
- Organization has published a homeland security selection data guide to support operational and strategic decision making.

☑ Approach   ☑ Deployment   ☑ Learning   ☑ Integration

4.1a(2) Organization selects and ensures the effective use of key homeland security comparative data and information to support operational and strategic decision making and innovation.

+ Strengths

1.

2.

3.

– Opportunities for Improvement

1.

2.

3.

Homeland Security Planning Issues:

Short Term (1 to 2 years)

1.

2.

Long Term (2 years or more)

1.

2.

4.1a(3) How does your organization keep its performance measurement system for homeland security current with business needs and directions?

Interview notes:

Zero-Based Preparation   **World-Class Preparation**

0	10	20	30	40	50	60	70	80	90	100

| Green | Blue | Yellow | Orange | Red |
| (Low) | (Guarded) | (Elevated) | (High) | (Severe) |

(Circle Appropriate Percentile)

Zero-Based Organization

- Organization does nothing to keep its performance measurement system for homeland security current with business needs and directions.

- Organization has no process in place to ensure that its performance measurement system for homeland security is timely and sensitive to unexpected external security changes.

World-Class Organization

- Organization reviews its performance measurement system for homeland security annually to ensure it remains current with business needs and directions.

- Organization ensures that its performance measurement system for homeland security is sensitive to rapid and unexpected security and emergency changes.

☑ Approach   ☑ Deployment   ☑ Learning   ☑ Integration

4.1a(3) Organization's performance measurement system for homeland security is kept current with business needs and directions.

+ Strengths

1.
2.
3.

– Opportunities for Improvement

1.
2.
3.

Homeland Security Planning Issues:

Short Term (1 to 2 years)

1.
2.

Long Term (2 years or more)

1.
2.

4.1b(1) What analysis does your organization perform to support senior leaders' organizational performance review and the organization's strategic planning for homeland security?

Interview notes:

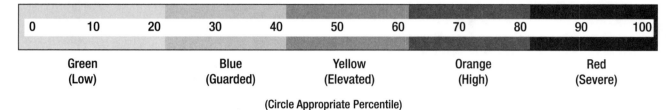

Zero-Based Preparation **World-Class Preparation**

| 0 | 10 | 20 | 30 | 40 | 50 | 60 | 70 | 80 | 90 | 100 |

Green (Low) Blue (Guarded) Yellow (Elevated) Orange (High) Red (Severe)

(Circle Appropriate Percentile)

Zero-Based Organization

- Organization uses anecdotal data to support senior leaders' organizational performance reviews and the organization's strategic planning for homeland security.
- Organization does not analyze data and information to support senior leaders' performance reviews for homeland security.

World-Class Organization

- Organization uses selected threat information to support senior leaders' organizational performance review and the organization's strategic planning for homeland security.
- Organization uses declassified national security information from state and federal agencies to support leadership's organizational performance review and strategic plans and goals.

☑ Approach   ☑ Deployment   ☑ Learning   ☑ Integration

4.1b(1) Organization performs analysis to support senior leaders' organizational performance review and the organization's strategic planning for homeland security.

+ Strengths
1.
2.
3.

– Opportunities for Improvement
1.
2.
3.

Homeland Security Planning Issues:

Short Term (1 to 2 years)
1.
2.

Long Term (2 years or more)
1.
2.

4.1b(2) How does your organization communicate the results of organizational-level homeland security analysis to work group and functional-level operations that enable effective support for decision making?

Interview notes:

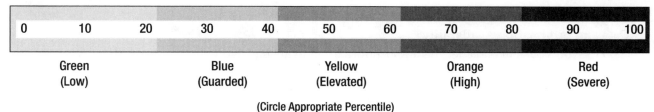

Zero-Based Preparation					World-Class Preparation

0   10   20   30   40   50   60   70   80   90   100

Green
(Low)
Blue
(Guarded)
Yellow
(Elevated)
Orange
(High)
Red
(Severe)

(Circle Appropriate Percentile)

Zero-Based Organization

- Organization's homeland security data are neither linked to nor supportive of work-group and functional-level decision making regarding corporate security issues.

- Organization does not communicate homeland security data to employees, suppliers, partners, and customers.

World-Class Organization

- Organization's homeland security data is user-friendly and presented in vivid graphs and charts to support functional-level decision making regarding security issues.

- Organization communicates homeland security organizational results through its online homeland security newsletters to employees, suppliers, partners, and customers.

☑ Approach   ☑ Deployment   ☑ Learning   ☑ Integration

4.1b(2) Organization communicates results of organizational-level homeland security analysis to work-group and functional-level operations that enable effective support for decision making.

+ Strengths
1.
2.
3.

– Opportunities for Improvement
1.
2.
3.

Homeland Security Planning Issues:

Short Term (1 to 2 years)
1.
2.

Long Term (2 years or more)
1.
2.

4.2 Information and Knowledge Management (45 pts.)

Describe how your organization ensures the quality and availability of needed data and information for employees, suppliers, partners, and customers. Describe how your organization builds and manages its knowledge assets.

AREAS TO ADDRESS

a. Data and Information Availability

(1) How do you make needed data and information available? How do you make them accessible to employees, suppliers, partners, and customers, as appropriate?

(2) How do you ensure that hardware and software are reliable, secure, and user-friendly?

(3) How do you keep your data and information availability mechanisms, including your software and hardware systems, current with business needs and directions?

b. Organizational Knowledge

(1) How do you manage organizational knowledge to accomplish:

- The collection and transfer of employee knowledge
- The transfer of relevant knowledge from customers, suppliers, and partners
- The identification and sharing of best practices

(2) How do you ensure the following properties of your data, information, and organizational knowledge:

- Integrity
- Timeliness
- Reliability
- Security
- Accuracy
- Confidentiality

4.2 Percent Score

 Approach   Deployment   Learning   Integration

4.2a(1) How does your organization ensure that needed homeland security data and information is available to employees, suppliers, partners, and customers?

Interview notes:

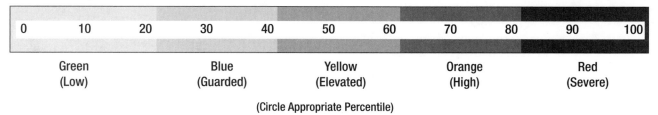

Zero-Based Preparation									World-Class Preparation
0	10	20	30	40	50	60	70	80	90	100

| Green (Low) | Blue (Guarded) | Yellow (Elevated) | Orange (High) | Red (Severe) |

(Circle Appropriate Percentile)

Zero-Based Organization

- Organization does not have a consistent and reliable method for deploying homeland security data and information to various stakeholders.
- Organization sends homeland security data and information on a "request only" basis to employees, suppliers, partners, and customers.

World-Class Organization

- Organization uses a subscriber website to deploy needed homeland security data and information to employees, suppliers, partners, and customers.
- Organization has a dedicated homeland security team to dispense needed homeland security data and information to suppliers, partners, and customers daily.

☑ Approach   ☑ Deployment   ☑ Learning   ☑ Integration

4.2a(1) Organization ensures that needed homeland security data and information is available to employees, suppliers, partners, and customers.

+ Strengths

1.

2.

3.

– Opportunities for Improvement

1.

2.

3.

Homeland Security Planning Issues:

Short Term (1 to 2 years)

1.

2.

Long Term (2 years or more)

1.

2.

4.2a(2) How does your organization ensure that hardware and software supporting homeland security is reliable, secure, and user-friendly?

Interview notes:

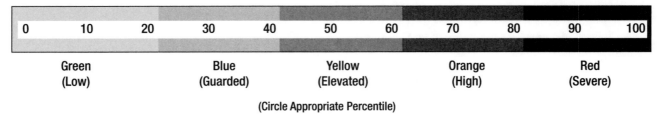

Zero-Based Preparation   **World-Class Preparation**

| 0 | 10 | 20 | 30 | 40 | 50 | 60 | 70 | 80 | 90 | 100 |

Green (Low) Blue (Guarded) Yellow (Elevated) Orange (High) Red (Severe)

(Circle Appropriate Percentile)

Zero-Based Organization

- Organization does not review its homeland security hardware/software to ensure reliability, security, and user-friendliness.
- Organization has no concern that hardware and software supporting homeland security are reliable, secure, and user-friendly.

World-Class Organization

- Organization has a committee in place to review homeland security hardware and software reliability, security, and user-friendliness semiannually.
- Organization surveys employees, suppliers, partners, and customers annually to gauge their satisfaction with homeland security data reliability, security, and user-friendliness.

☑ Approach   ☑ Deployment   ☑ Learning   ☑ Integration

4.2a(2) Organization ensures that hardware and software supporting homeland security is reliable, secure, and user-friendly.

+ Strengths
1.
2.
3.

– Opportunities for Improvement
1.
2.
3.

Homeland Security Planning Issues:

Short Term (1 to 2 years)
1.
2.

Long Term (2 years or more)
1.
2.

4.2a(3) How does your organization keep data and information availability mechanisms that support homeland security, including software and hardware systems, current with business needs and directions?

Interview notes:

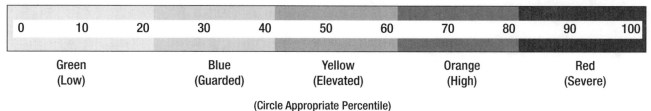

| Zero-Based Preparation | | | | | | | | | | World-Class Preparation |

| 0 | 10 | 20 | 30 | 40 | 50 | 60 | 70 | 80 | 90 | 100 |

| Green (Low) | | Blue (Guarded) | | Yellow (Elevated) | | Orange (High) | | Red (Severe) | |

(Circle Appropriate Percentile)

Zero-Based Organization

- Organization has no infrastructure in place to support information networks for homeland security.
- Organization has little concern that systems are in place to support homeland security data and information.

World-Class Organization

- Organization benchmarks notable "best practice" information systems that support homeland security to ensure that its system is current with business needs and directions.
- Organization has in place a homeland security data support team to ensure that software/hardware systems are current with the organization's security needs.

☑ Approach   ☑ Deployment   ☑ Learning   ☑ Integration

4.2a(3) Organization keeps data and information availability mechanisms that support homeland security, including software and hardware systems, current with business needs and directions.

+ Strengths

1.

2.

3.

– Opportunities for Improvement

1.

2.

3.

Homeland Security Planning Issues:

Short Term (1 to 2 years)

1.

2.

Long Term (2 years or more)

1.

2.

4.2b(1) How does your organization collect and transfer relevant organizational knowledge and sharing of best practices that relates to homeland security to and from employees, customers, suppliers, and partners?

Interview notes:

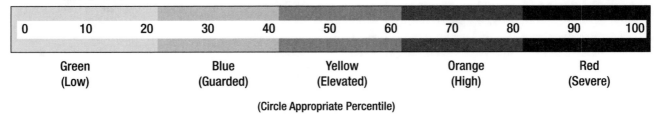

Zero-Based Preparation   World-Class Preparation

| 0 | 10 | 20 | 30 | 40 | 50 | 60 | 70 | 80 | 90 | 100 |

| Green (Low) | Blue (Guarded) | Yellow (Elevated) | Orange (High) | Red (Severe) |

(Circle Appropriate Percentile)

Zero-Based Organization

- Organization has no systematic methodology in place to manage, collect, and transfer homeland security knowledge and best practices.
- Organization collects homeland security data and information but has no system in place to store and transfer knowledge to stakeholder groups.

World-Class Organization

- Organization has a software system in place that manages, collects, and transfers homeland security data and information and best practices to employees, suppliers, partners, and customers.
- Organization has an online knowledge management system for homeland security that is accessible to employees, suppliers, partners, and customers.

☑ Approach   ☑ Deployment   ☑ Learning   ☑ Integration

4.2b(1) Organization collects and transfers relevant organizational knowledge and sharing of best practices that relates to homeland security to and from employees, customers, suppliers, and partners.

+ Strengths

1.
2.
3.

– Opportunities for Improvement

1.
2.
3.

Homeland Security Planning Issues:

Short Term (1 to 2 years)

1.
2.

Long Term (2 years or more)

1.
2.

4.2b(2) How does your organization ensure that its homeland security data, information, and organizational knowledge have integrity and are timely, reliable, secure, accurate, and confidential?

Interview notes:

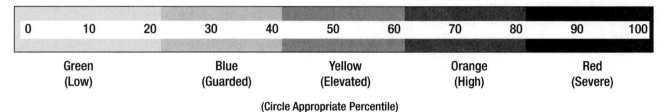

Zero-Based Preparation   **World-Class Preparation**

| 0 | 10 | 20 | 30 | 40 | 50 | 60 | 70 | 80 | 90 | 100 |

| Green
(Low) | Blue
(Guarded) | Yellow
(Elevated) | Orange
(High) | Red
(Severe) |

(Circle Appropriate Percentile)

Zero-Based Organization	**World-Class Organization**
• Organization has no process in place to ensure that data and knowledge management are reliable, protected, timely, and secure. • Organization has no ongoing systems in place to review and ensure that homeland security data, information, and organizational knowledge are maintained properly.	• Organization surveys data users bimonthly to ensure homeland security data and knowledge management have integrity, timeliness, reliability, security, accuracy, and confidentiality. • Organization's homeland security data, information, and organizational knowledge are reviewed weekly to ensure that it is reliable, protected, timely, and secure.

☑ Approach ☑ Deployment ☑ Learning ☑ Integration

4.2b(2) Organization ensures that homeland security data, information, and organizational knowledge has integrity and is timely, reliable, secure, accurate, and confidential.

+ Strengths

1.

2.

3.

– Opportunities for Improvement

1.

2.

3.

Homeland Security Planning Issues:

Short Term (1 to 2 years)

1.

2.

Long Term (2 years or more)

1.

2.

Notes

7

Category 5
Human Resource
Focus

5 Human Resource Focus (85 pts.)[14]

The Human Resource Focus Category examines how your organization's work systems and employee learning and motivation enable employees to develop and use their full potential in alignment with your organization's overall homeland security objectives and action plans. Also examined are your organization's efforts to build and maintain a work environment and employee support climate conducive to performance excellence and to personal and organizational growth that supports the organization's homeland security plans and goals.

 Forms can be downloaded from the CD-ROM located inside the back cover of this book.

5.1 Work Systems (35 pts.)

Process

Describe how your organization's work and jobs enable employees and the organization to achieve high performance. Describe how compensation, career progression, and related workforce practices enable employees and the organization to achieve high performance.

AREAS TO ADDRESS

a. Organization and Management of Work

(1) How do you organize and manage work and jobs to promote cooperation, initiative, empowerment innovation, and your organizational culture? How do you organize and manage work and jobs to achieve the agility to keep current with business needs?

(2) How do your work systems capitalize on the diverse ideas, cultures, and thinking of your employees and the communities with which you interact (your employee hiring and your customer communities)?

(3) How do you achieve effective communication and skill sharing across work units, jobs, and locations?

b. Employee Performance Management System

How does your employee performance management system, including feedback to employees, support high performance? How does your employee performance management system support a customer and business focus? How do your compensation, recognition, and related reward and incentive practices reinforce high-performance work and a customer and business focus?

c. Hiring and Career Progression

(1) How do you identify characteristics and skills needed by potential employees?

(2) How do you recruit, hire, and retain new employees? How do you ensure that the employees represent the diverse ideas, cultures, and thinking of your employee hiring community?

(3) How do you accomplish effective succession planning for leadership and management positions, including senior leadership? How do you manage effective career progression for all employees throughout the organization?

5.1 Percent
Score

 Approach   Deployment   ✔ Learning   ✔ Integration

5.1a(1) How does your organization structure and manage work and jobs to promote cooperation, initiative, empowerment, and innovation to achieve the agility needed to address homeland security initiatives within the organization?

Interview notes:

Zero-Based Preparation   **World-Class Preparation**

0	10	20	30	40	50	60	70	80	90	100

Green (Low)   Blue (Guarded)   Yellow (Elevated)   Orange (High)   Red (Severe)

(Circle Appropriate Percentile)

Zero-Based Organization

- No systematic process is in place to design, organize, and manage homeland security work and jobs for employees that promote cooperation, empowerment, innovation, and collaboration.
- Organization does not address work system structure that promotes cooperation and collaboration of employees and meets homeland security needs.

World-Class Organization

- Organization conducts an annual work system review to ensure that employees' cooperation and collaboration meet the organization's homeland security plans and goals.
- Employees are grouped into various work teams (e.g., safety teams, cross-functional teams) to promote cooperation and collaboration to keep current the organization's homeland security needs and directions.

✔ Approach   ✔ Deployment   ✔ Learning   ✔ Integration

5.1a(1) Organization structures and manages work and jobs to promote cooperation, initiative, empowerment, and innovation to achieve the agility needed to address homeland security initiatives.

+ Strengths
1.
2.
3.

– Opportunities for Improvement
1.
2.
3.

Homeland Security Planning Issues:

Short Term (1 to 2 years)
1.
2.

Long Term (2 years or more)
1.
2.

5.1a(2) How do your organization's work systems capitalize on the diverse ideas, cultures, and thinking of employees regarding homeland security issues?

Interview notes:

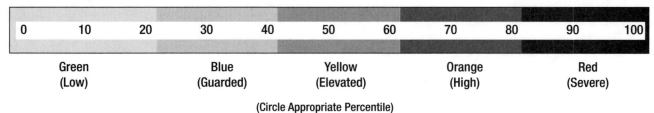

Zero-Based Organization

- Organization's work systems are not formalized and do not capitalize on diverse thinking among employees regarding homeland security.
- Organization's work systems do not support employee interaction regarding homeland security issues.

World-Class Organization

- Organization's homeland security work teams, process teams, and peer coaching teams promote diverse ideas and thinking throughout the organization about homeland security issues and vulnerabilities.
- Organization promotes cross-functional teams among employees to capitalize on their diverse ideas, cultures, and diverse thinking to identify homeland security issues and vulnerabilities.

☑ Approach ☑ Deployment ☑ Learning ☑ Integration

5.1a(2) Organization's work systems capitalize on the diverse ideas, cultures, and thinking of employees regarding homeland security issues.

+ Strengths

1.
2.
3.

– Opportunities for Improvement

1.
2.
3.

Homeland Security Planning Issues:

Short Term (1 to 2 years)

1.
2.

Long Term (2 years or more)

1.
2.

5.1a(3) How does your organization achieve effective communication and skill sharing across work units, jobs, and locations regarding homeland security issues?

Interview notes:

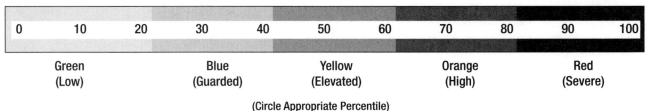

Zero-Based Preparation   **World-Class Preparation**

| 0 | 10 | 20 | 30 | 40 | 50 | 60 | 70 | 80 | 90 | 100 |

| Green
(Low) | Blue
(Guarded) | Yellow
(Elevated) | Orange
(High) | Red
(Severe) |

(Circle Appropriate Percentile)

Zero-Based Organization

- Organization has no process in place to ensure effective communication, cooperation, and knowledge/skill sharing among employees regarding homeland security.
- Homeland security knowledge/skill sharing among employees is not encouraged by the organization's leadership.

World-Class Organization

- Organization requires all cross-functional teams to share their homeland security project results on the organization's password-protected intranet.
- Organization promotes the use of e-mail and in-house workshops for employees to communicate and share homeland security knowledge and skills organization-wide.

☑ Approach   ☑ Deployment   ☑ Learning   ☑ Integration

5.1a(3) Organization achieves effective communication and skill sharing across work units, jobs, and locations regarding homeland security issues.

+ Strengths

1.

2.

3.

– Opportunities for Improvement

1.

2.

3.

Homeland Security Planning Issues:

Short Term (1 to 2 years)

1.

2.

Long Term (2 years or more)

1.

2.

5.1b How does your organization's employee performance management system, including feedback from employees, support homeland security initiatives within the organization?

Interview notes:

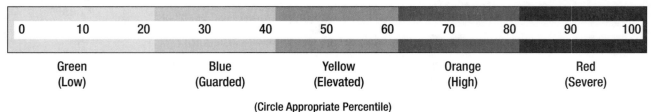

Zero-Based Preparation   World-Class Preparation

| 0 | 10 | 20 | 30 | 40 | 50 | 60 | 70 | 80 | 90 | 100 |

Green   Blue   Yellow   Orange   Red
(Low)   (Guarded)   (Elevated)   (High)   (Severe)

(Circle Appropriate Percentile)

Zero-Based Organization

- Organization's management system does not support or promote addressing homeland security issues among employees.
- Organization allows only senior management to be involved with and support homeland security initiatives.

World-Class Organization

- Organization groups employees into cross-functional teams to promote homeland security awareness among employees. Each team collects data that may be used to gauge performance results of homeland security initiatives.
- Organization's performance management system supports and recognizes employee involvement and support for its homeland security efforts.

[✔] Approach   [✔] Deployment   [✔] Learning   [✔] Integration

5.1b Organization's employee performance management system supports homeland security initiatives within the organization.

+ Strengths
1.
2.
3.

– Opportunities for Improvement
1.
2.
3.

Homeland Security Planning Issues:

Short Term (1 to 2 years)
1.
2.

Long Term (2 years or more)
1.
2.

5.1c(1) How does your organization identify characteristics and skills, needed by potential employees, that safeguard homeland security within the organization?

Interview notes:

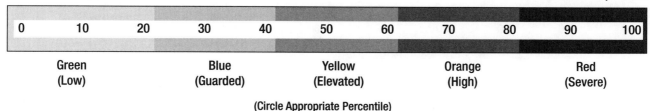

Zero-Based Preparation   **World-Class Preparation**

| 0 | 10 | 20 | 30 | 40 | 50 | 60 | 70 | 80 | 90 | 100 |

| Green (Low) | Blue (Guarded) | Yellow (Elevated) | Orange (High) | Red (Severe) |

(Circle Appropriate Percentile)

Zero-Based Organization

- Organization has no process in place to identify characteristics and skills needed by potential employees and has no concern for identifying characteristics and skills they need to ensure a safe work environment and promote homeland security.

- Organization has no concern for identifying characteristics and skills of potential employees who may breach homeland security.

World-Class Organization

- Organization has in place a documented list of characteristics and skills required of potential employees. Organization has aligned identified security threat characteristics of potential employees obtained from benchmark findings of several agencies to ensure a safe work environment and to promote homeland security.

- Organization uses a list of characteristics and skills, secured from federal agencies, to help identify potential employees who may pose a security risk to the organization.

☑ **Approach**   ☑ **Deployment**   ☑ **Learning**   ☑ **Integration**

5.1c(1) Organization identifies characteristics and skills needed by potential employees that safeguard homeland security within the organization.

+ Strengths

1.

2.

3.

– Opportunities for Improvement

1.

2.

3.

Homeland Security Planning Issues:

Short Term (1 to 2 years)

1.

2.

Long Term (2 years or more)

1.

2.

5.1c(2) How does your organization recruit, hire, and retain new employees and ensure a safe work environment for homeland security within the organization?

Interview notes:

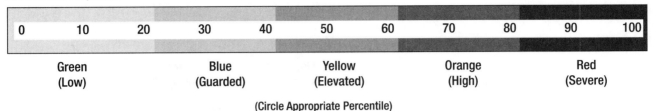

| 0 | 10 | 20 | 30 | 40 | 50 | 60 | 70 | 80 | 90 | 100 |

Green
(Low)

Blue
(Guarded)

Yellow
(Elevated)

Orange
(High)

Red
(Severe)

(Circle Appropriate Percentile)

Zero-Based Organization

- Organization has no consistent homeland security policies or procedures that address recruiting, hiring, and retaining new employees.
- Organization has not addressed homeland security issues for potential and newly hired employees.

World-Class Organization

- Organization has documented procedures in place that address recruiting, hiring, and retaining new employees to ensure a safe work environment for homeland security.
- Organization has developed a homeland security orientation program for potential and newly hired employees that promotes workplace safety and security.

☑ Approach   ☑ Deployment   ☑ Learning   ☑ Integration

5.1c(2) Organization recruits, hires, and retains new employees and ensures a safe work environment for homeland security within the organization.

+ Strengths
1.
2.
3.

– Opportunities for Improvement
1.
2.
3.

Homeland Security Planning Issues:

Short Term (1 to 2 years)
1.
2.

Long Term (2 years or more)
1.
2.

5.1c(3) How does your organization accomplish effective succession planning for leadership and management and ensure that they promote a safe work environment for homeland security within the organization?

Interview notes:

Zero-Based Preparation   **World-Class Preparation**

0	10	20	30	40	50	60	70	80	90	100

Green (Low)	Blue (Guarded)	Yellow (Elevated)	Orange (High)	Red (Severe)

(Circle Appropriate Percentile)

Zero-Based Organization

- Organization does nothing to accomplish effective succession planning among senior staff and supervisory positions and to promote its support for homeland security initiatives.

- Organization has limited succession planning for senior leadership and supervisory positions and does not align homeland security issues with promotability.

World-Class Organization

- Organization manages career progression and succession planning of senior leadership and supervisory positions through a formal mentoring program and career development plan. Positions are rotated every two years to help build the career knowledge base among senior and supervisory staff and to promote support for homeland security issues within the organization.

- Organization's succession planning for leadership and management positions is aligned with its involvement with homeland security initiatives throughout the organization.

☑ Approach   ☑ Deployment   ☑ Learning   ☑ Integration

5.1c(3) Organization's succession planning for leadership and management ensures that they will promote a safe work environment for homeland security within the organization.

+ Strengths

1.
2.
3.

– Opportunities for Improvement

1.
2.
3.

Homeland Security Planning Issues:

Short Term (1 to 2 years)

1.
2.

Long Term (2 years or more)

1.
2.

5.2 Employee Learning and Motivation (25 pts.)

Describe how your organization's employee education, training, and career development support the achievement of your overall objectives and contribute to high performance. Describe how your organization's education, training, and career development build employee knowledge, skills, and capabilities.

AREAS TO ADDRESS

a. Employee Education, Training, and Development

(1) How do employee education and training contribute to the achievement of your action plans? How do your employee education, training, and development address your key needs associated with organizational performance measurement, performance improvement, and technological change? How does your education and training approach balance short- and longer-term organizational objectives with employee needs for development, learning, and career progression?

(2) How do employee education, training, and development address your key organizational needs associated with new employee orientation, diversity, ethical business practices, and management and leadership development? How do employee education, training, and development address your key organizational needs associated with employee, workplace, and environmental safety?

(3) How do you seek and use input from employees and their supervisors and managers on education and training needs? How do you incorporate your organizational learning and knowledge assets into your education and training?

(4) How do you deliver education and training? How do you seek and use input from employees and their supervisors and managers on options for the delivery of education and training? How do you use both formal and informal delivery approaches, including mentoring and other approaches, as appropriate?

(5) How do you reinforce the use of new knowledge and skills on the job?

(6) How do you evaluate the effectiveness of education and training, taking into account individual and organizational performance?

b. Motivation and Career Development

How do you motivate employees to develop and use their full potential? How does your organization use formal and informal mechanisms to help employees attain job- and careerrelated development and learning objectives? How do managers and supervisors help employees attain job- and career-related development and learning objectives?

5.2 Percent Score

 Approach   Deployment   Learning   ☑ Integration

5.2a(1) How do your organization's employee education and training contribute to the achievement of a safe work environment and the accomplishment of homeland security action plans?

Interview notes:

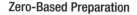

Zero-Based Preparation   **World-Class Preparation**

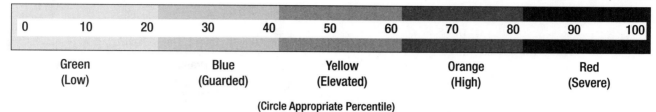

| Green | Blue | Yellow | Orange | Red |
| (Low) | (Guarded) | (Elevated) | (High) | (Severe) |

(Circle Appropriate Percentile)

Zero-Based Organization

- Organization's education and training do not support key homeland security strategic goals.
- Organization has limited training that contributes to the achievement of a safe work environment and helps accomplish homeland security action plans.

World-Class Organization

- Organization's employee training and development needs are integrated with its short- and long-term homeland security strategic plans and goals.
- Organization's employee workshops and training programs address topics that support its key strategic homeland security goals and action plans.

☑ Approach   ☑ Deployment   ☑ Learning   ☑ Integration

5.2a(1) Organization's employee education and training contribute to the achievement of a safe work environment and the accomplishment of homeland security action plans.

+ Strengths

1.

2.

3.

– Opportunities for Improvement

1.

2.

3.

Homeland Security Planning Issues:

Short Term (1 to 2 years)

1.

2.

Long Term (2 years or more)

1.

2.

5.2a(2) How do your organization's education, training, and development address key homeland security needs associated with new employee orientation, training and development, and workplace and environmental safety?

Interview notes:

Zero-Based Preparation   **World-Class Preparation**

| 0 | 10 | 20 | 30 | 40 | 50 | 60 | 70 | 80 | 90 | 100 |

| Green
(Low) | | Blue
(Guarded) | | Yellow
(Elevated) | | Orange
(High) | | Red
(Severe) |

(Circle Appropriate Percentile)

Zero-Based Organization

- Organization conducts very little homeland security training for employees and has no formal training design in place.
- Organization conducts on-the-job training (OJT) for homeland security as needed. No systematic design proess is in place for employees that supports overall homeland security needs and objectives.

World-Class Organization

- Organization has a curriculum development team in place that is made up of selected employees and various stakeholders to design and evaluate education and training to support overall homeland security needs and objectives.
- Organization identifies and has a design methodology in place to deploy on-the-job training (OJT) supporting its homeland security goals and objectives.

☑ **Approach**　　☑ **Deployment**　　☑ **Learning**　　☑ **Integration**

5.2a(2) Organization's education, training, and development address key homeland security needs associated with new employee orientation, training and development, and workplace and environmental safety.

+ Strengths
1.
2.
3.

– Opportunities for Improvement
1.
2.
3.

Homeland Security Planning Issues:

Short Term (1 to 2 years)
1.
2.

Long Term (2 years or more)
1.
2.

5.2a(3) How does your organization seek and use input from employees and their supervisors and managers on homeland security education and training needs?

Interview notes:

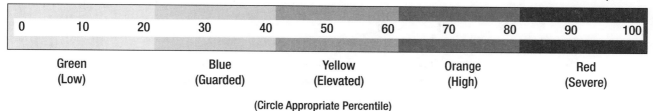

Zero-Based Preparation   **World-Class Preparation**

| 0 | 10 | 20 | 30 | 40 | 50 | 60 | 70 | 80 | 90 | 100 |

| Green | Blue | Yellow | Orange | Red |
| (Low) | (Guarded) | (Elevated) | (High) | (Severe) |

(Circle Appropriate Percentile)

Zero-Based Organization

- Organization's employees, senior leaders, and supervisors are not involved with contributing to the training and curriculum design for its homeland security efforts.

- A professional homeland security training group develops all training and education design without receiving input from senior leaders, supervisors, and employees.

World-Class Organization

- Organization involves employees, senior leaders, and supervisors in focus groups to identify homeland security training needs. Findings are used for curriculum design.

- Organization's homeland security training and curriculum design involves representatives from employees, senior leadership, supervisory staff, key suppliers, partners, and customers.

✔ Approach   ✔ Deployment   ✔ Learning   ✔ Integration

5.2a(3) Organization seeks and uses input from employees and their supervisors and managers on homeland security education and training needs.

+ Strengths

1.

2.

3.

– Opportunities for Improvement

1.

2.

3.

Homeland Security Planning Issues:

Short Term (1 to 2 years)

1.

2.

Long Term (2 years or more)

1.

2.

5.2a(4) How does your organization deliver homeland security education and training?

Interview notes:

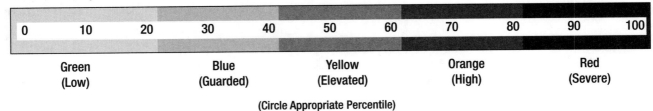

Zero-Based Preparation   **World-Class Preparation**

| 0 | 10 | 20 | 30 | 40 | 50 | 60 | 70 | 80 | 90 | 100 |

Green
(Low)   Blue
(Guarded)   Yellow
(Elevated)   Orange
(High)   Red
(Severe)

(Circle Appropriate Percentile)

Zero-Based Organization

- Organization has not identified a consistent delivery method for its homeland security education and training and does not gauge delivery method results.
- Organization is not concerned with how education and training are delivered.

World-Class Organization

- Organization delivers homeland security training and education through classrooms, on-the-job, computer-based, and distance learning.
- Organization has a formal mentoring process in place to train new employees and to reinforce existing training initiatives on its homeland security issues.

☑ Approach   ☑ Deployment   ☑ Learning   ☑ Integration

5.2a(4) Organization delivers homeland security education and training.

+ Strengths

1.
2.
3.

– Opportunities for Improvement

1.
2.
3.

Homeland Security Planning Issues:

Short Term (1 to 2 years)

1.
2.

Long Term (2 years or more)

1.
2.

5.2a(5) How does your organization reinforce the use of new homeland security knowledge and skills on the job?

Interview notes:

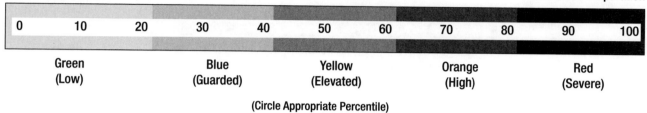

Zero-Based Preparation   **World-Class Preparation**

| 0 | 10 | 20 | 30 | 40 | 50 | 60 | 70 | 80 | 90 | 100 |

Green (Low)   Blue (Guarded)   Yellow (Elevated)   Orange (High)   Red (Severe)

(Circle Appropriate Percentile)

Zero-Based Organization

- Organization has no process in place to ensure that homeland security knowledge and skills received by employees in training sessions has on-the-job application.
- Organization is not concerned about on-thejob application of new homeland security knowledge received by employees.

World-Class Organization

- Organization has an evaluation process in place to ensure that new homeland security knowledge received by employees in training sessions has on-the-job application.
- In the organization's monthly newsletter, senior leadership recognizes employees who apply new homeland security knowledge and skills received through training on the job.

☑ Approach   ☑ Deployment   ☑ Learning   ☑ Integration

5.2a(5) Organization reinforces the use of new homeland security knowledge and skills on the job.

+ Strengths
1.
2.
3.

– Opportunities for Improvement
1.
2.
3.

Homeland Security Planning Issues:

Short Term (1 to 2 years)
1.
2.

Long Term (2 years or more)
1.
2.

5.2a(6) How does your organization evaluate the effectiveness of homeland security education and training?

Interview notes:

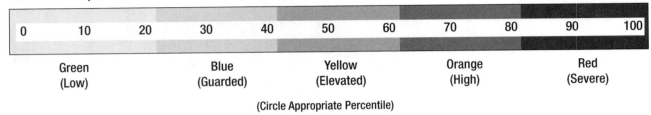

Zero-Based Preparation   **World-Class Preparation**

0   10   20   30   40   50   60   70   80   90   100

Green   Blue   Yellow   Orange   Red
(Low)   (Guarded)   (Elevated)   (High)   (Severe)

(Circle Appropriate Percentile)

Zero-Based Organization

- Organization has no process in place to improve its education and training effectiveness for homeland security.
- Organization ensures that education and training is conducted for homeland security, but does not evaluate this training.

World-Class Organization

- Organization has a formal evaluation process for all homeland security training and education that is delivered. Each training session receives participant evaluation, and findings are used for curriculum improvement.
- Organization evaluates on-the-job application of all homeland security training and education delivered to employees. A team reviews all on-the-job applications and uses input to improve education and training.

☑ Approach   ☑ Deployment   ☑ Learning   ☑ Integration

5.2a(6) Organization evaluates the effectiveness of homeland security education and training.

+ Strengths
1.
2.
3.

– Opportunities for Improvement
1.
2.
3.

Homeland Security Planning Issues:

Short Term (1 to 2 years)
1.
2.

Long Term (2 years or more)
1.
2.

5.2b How does your organization motivate employees to develop and use their full potential to ensure a safe and secure environment?

Interview notes:

Zero-Based Preparation   **World-Class Preparation**

| 0 | 10 | 20 | 30 | 40 | 50 | 60 | 70 | 80 | 90 | 100 |

Green
(Low)

Blue
(Guarded)

Yellow
(Elevated)

Orange
(High)

Red
(Severe)

(Circle Appropriate Percentile)

Zero-Based Organization

- Organization has no processes in place to motivate employees to develop and use their full potential to ensure a safe and secure work environment.
- Organization has no concern for motivating employees to develop their knowledge and skills to ensure a safe and secure work environment.

World-Class Organization

- Organization has developed a leadership academy for homeland security to motivate employees to attain job- and career-related development and to use their full potential to ensure a safe and secure work environment.
- Organization has a formal recognition program in place that motivates and rewards employees to develop and use their full potential in ensuring a safe and secure work environment.

☑ Approach   ☑ Deployment   ☑ Learning   ☑ Integration

5.2b Organization motivates employees to develop and use their full potential to ensure a safe and secure work environment.

+ Strengths
1.
2.
3.

– Opportunities for Improvement
1.
2.
3.

Homeland Security Planning Issues:

Short Term (1 to 2 years)
1.
2.

Long Term (2 years or more)
1.
2.

5.3 Employee Well-Being and Satisfaction (25 pts.)

Describe how your organization maintains a work environment and an employee support climate that contribute to the well-being, satisfaction, and motivation of all employees.

AREAS TO ADDRESS

a. **Work Environment**

    (1) How do you improve workplace health, safety, security, and ergonomics? How do employees take part in improving them? What are your performance measures or targets for each of these key workplace factors? What are the significant differences in workplace factors and performance measures or targets if different employee groups and work units have different work environments?

    (2) How do you ensure workplace preparedness for emergencies or disasters? How do you seek to ensure business continuity for the benefit of your employees and customers?

b. **Employee Support and Satisfaction**

    (1) How do you determine the key factors that affect employee well-being, satisfaction, and motivation? How are these factors segmented for a diverse workforce and for different categories and types of employees?

    (2) How do you support your employees via services, benefits, and policies? How are these tailored to the needs of a diverse workforce and different categories and types of employees?

    (3) What formal and informal assessment methods and measures do you use to determine employee well-being, satisfaction, and motivation? How do these methods and measures differ across a diverse workforce and different categories and types of employees? How do you use other indicators, such as employee retention, absenteeism, grievances, safety, and productivity, to assess and improve employee well-being, satisfaction, and motivation?

    (4) How do you relate assessment findings to key business results to identify priorities for improving the work environment and employee support climate?

5.3 Percent Score

 Approach   Deployment   Learning   Integration

5.3a(1) How does your organization improve workplace health, safety, and security through homeland security efforts and initiatives?

Interview notes:

Zero-Based Preparation   **World-Class Preparation**

0	10	20	30	40	50	60	70	80	90	100

Green
(Low)

Blue
(Guarded)

Yellow
(Elevated)

Orange
(High)

Red
(Severe)

(Circle Appropriate Percentile)

Zero-Based Organization

- Organization does nothing to maintain a safe, secure, and healthful work environment.
- Organization's leadership has no concern for maintaining an environment that is safe, secure, and healthful and that supports the well-being, satisfaction, and motivation of employees.

World-Class Organization

- Organization surveys employees to determine to what extent the work environment supports their safety and health. Findings are used to address areas of concern regarding homeland security.
- Organization provides counseling to employees regarding safety, security, and health issues that are related to homeland security.

☑ Approach   ☑ Deployment   ☑ Learning   ☑ Integration

5.3a(1) Organization improves workplace health, safety, and security through its homeland security efforts and initiatives.

+ Strengths
1.
2.
3.

– Opportunities for Improvement
1.
2.
3.

Homeland Security Planning Issues:

Short Term (1 to 2 years)
1.
2.

Long Term (2 years or more)
1.
2.

5.3a(2) How does your organization ensure workplace preparedness for homeland security emergencies or disasters?

Interview notes:

Zero-Based Preparation   **World-Class Preparation**

| 0 | 10 | 20 | 30 | 40 | 50 | 60 | 70 | 80 | 90 | 100 |

Green   Blue   Yellow   Orange   Red
(Low)   (Guarded)   (Elevated)   (High)   (Severe)

(Circle Appropriate Percentile)

Zero-Based Organization

- Organization has no emergency and/or disaster plans in place for homeland security.
- Organization does not have documented procedures identified for workplace preparedness and homeland security.

World-Class Organization

- Organization has documented homeland security emergency and disaster plans in place and conducts periodic disaster drills for employees.
- Organization involves and trains employees and stakeholders in its workplace preparedness emergency and disaster plans for homeland security.

☑ **Approach**   ☑ **Deployment**   ☑ **Learning**   ☑ **Integration**

5.3a(2) Organization ensures workplace preparedness for homeland security emergencies or disasters.

+ Strengths

1.

2.

3.

– Opportunities for Improvement

1.

2.

3.

Homeland Security Planning Issues:

Short Term (1 to 2 years)

1.

2.

Long Term (2 years or more)

1.

2.

5.3b(1) How does your organization determine key homeland security factors that affect employee well-being, satisfaction, and motivation?

Interview notes:

Zero-Based Preparation   **World-Class Preparation**

| 0 | 10 | 20 | 30 | 40 | 50 | 60 | 70 | 80 | 90 | 100 |

| Green (Low) | Blue (Guarded) | Yellow (Elevated) | Orange (High) | Red (Severe) |

(Circle Appropriate Percentile)

Zero-Based Organization

- Organization has limited processes in place to holistically gauge key factors that affect employee well-being, satisfaction, and motivation regarding homeland security issues.
- Organization has no concern for determining key factors that affect the employee work environment and homeland security issues.

World-Class Organization

- Organization conducts an annual employee climate survey that segments the diverse workforce to determine key factors that affect employee well-being, satisfaction, and motivation regarding homeland security issues.
- Organization has a formal grievance procedure that is used to determine key factors affecting the employee work environment regarding homeland security issues.

☑ Approach   ☑ Deployment   ☑ Learning   ☑ Integration

5.3b(1) Organization determines key homeland security factors that affect employee well-being, satisfaction, and motivation.

+ Strengths

1.

2.

3.

– Opportunities for Improvement

1.

2.

3.

Homeland Security Planning Issues:

Short Term (1 to 2 years)

1.

2.

Long Term (2 years or more)

1.

2.

5.3b(2) How does your organization support employee homeland security efforts via services, benefits, and policies?

Interview notes:

Zero-Based Preparation   **World-Class Preparation**

| 0 | 10 | 20 | 30 | 40 | 50 | 60 | 70 | 80 | 90 | 100 |

Green (Low)   Blue (Guarded)   Yellow (Elevated)   Orange (High)   Red (Severe)

(Circle Appropriate Percentile)

Zero-Based Organization

- Organization offers very limited special services for employees who support its homeland security efforts.
- Organization does not provide services, benefits, and policies for employees to support homeland security efforts.

World-Class Organization

- Organization provides special services and benefits for employees who support its homeland security efforts (e.g., off-site homeland security seminars, benchmarking tours, etc.).
- Organization's focus groups are conducted quarterly to discuss and identify special services and benefits that would aid employee well-being and satisfaction regarding homeland security issues.

☑ Approach   ☑ Deployment   ☑ Learning   ☑ Integration

5.3b(2) Organization supports employee homeland security efforts via services, benefits, and policies.

+ Strengths

1.
2.
3.

− Opportunities for Improvement

1.
2.
3.

Homeland Security Planning Issues:

Short Term (1 to 2 years)

1.
2.

Long Term (2 years or more)

1.
2.

5.3b(3) What are your organization's formal and informal assessment methods and measures to determine employee well-being, satisfaction, and motivation regarding the organization's homeland security efforts and initiatives?

Interview notes:

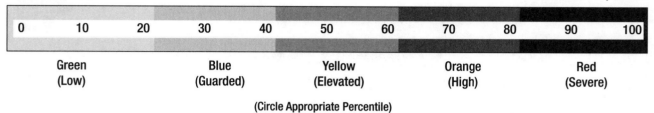

<table>
<tr><td>Zero-Based Preparation</td><td>World-Class Preparation</td></tr>
</table>

0   10   20   30   40   50   60   70   80   90   100

Green (Low)   Blue (Guarded)   Yellow (Elevated)   Orange (High)   Red (Severe)

(Circle Appropriate Percentile)

Zero-Based Organization

- Organization conducts no employee surveys or focus groups to determine well-being and satisfaction among employees regarding the organization's homeland security initiatives.
- Organization's senior leaders are unaware of employee morale issues and have no process in place to gauge their well-being and satisfaction with homeland security initiatives.

World-Class Organization

- Organization conducts an annual employee survey to determine employees' well-being and satisfaction with homeland security issues.
- Organization conducts employee focus groups to gauge their satisfaction and well-being with regard to homeland security initiatives within the organization.

✔ Approach   ✔ Deployment   ✔ Learning   ✔ Integration

5.3b(3) Organization's formal and informal assessment methods and measures to determine employee well-being, satisfaction, and motivation regarding homeland security efforts and initiatives.

+ Strengths

1.

2.

3.

– Opportunities for Improvement

1.

2.

3.

Homeland Security Planning Issues:

Short Term (1 to 2 years)

1.

2.

Long Term (2 years or more)

1.

2.

5.3b(4) How does your organization relate assessment findings to key homeland security results and use findings to identify priorities for improvement in the work environment?

Interview notes:
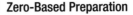

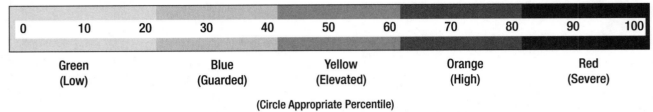

Zero-Based Preparation   **World-Class Preparation**

| 0 | 10 | 20 | 30 | 40 | 50 | 60 | 70 | 80 | 90 | 100 |

| Green | Blue | Yellow | Orange | Red |
| (Low) | (Guarded) | (Elevated) | (High) | (Severe) |

(Circle Appropriate Percentile)

Zero-Based Organization

- Organization's employee homeland security satisfaction and well-being data are not considered within the organization's strategic planning process.
- Organization makes no benchmark comparisons of employee satisfaction with homeland security initiatives against comparable organization's results.

World-Class Organization

- Organization's employee satisfaction and morale survey data is integrated into its planning process and findings used to identify priorities for homeland security issues.
- Organization uses its annual employee satisfaction results to identify work environment safety and security improvement priorities that support its homeland security plans and goals.

☑ Approach   ☑ Deployment   ☑ Learning   ☑ Integration

5.3b(4) Organization relates assessment findings to key homeland security results and uses findings to identify priorities for improvement in the work environment.

+ Strengths

1.

2.

3.

– Opportunities for Improvement

1.

2.

3.

Homeland Security Planning Issues:

Short Term (1 to 2 years)

1.

2.

Long Term (2 years or more)

1.

2.

Notes

8

Category 6
Process
Management

6 Process Management (85 pts.)[15]

The Process Management Category examines the key aspects of your organization's process management for homeland security initiatives, including key product, service, and business processes for creating customer and organizational value and key support processes. This category encompasses all key processes and all work units that address homeland security issues.

 Forms can be downloaded from the CD-ROM located inside the back cover of this book.

119

6.1 Value Creation Processes (50 pts.)

Describe how your organization identifies and manages its key processes for creating customer value and achieving business success and growth.

Process

AREAS TO ADDRESS

a. **Value Creation Processes**

(1) How does your organization determine its key value creation processes? What are your organization's key product, service, and business processes for creating or adding value? How do these processes create value for the organization, your customers, and your other key stakeholders? How do they contribute to profitability and business success?

(2) How do you determine key value creation process requirements, incorporating input from customers, suppliers, and partners, as appropriate? What are the key requirements for these processes?

(3) How do you design these processes to meet all the key requirements? How do you incorporate new technology and organizational knowledge into the design of these processes? How do you incorporate cycle time, productivity, cost control, and other efficiency and effectiveness factors into the design of these processes? How do you implement these processes to ensure they meet design requirements?

(4) What are your key performance measures or indicators used for the control and improvement of your value creation processes? How does your day-to-day operation of these processes ensure meeting key process requirements? How are in-process measures used in managing these processes? How is customer, supplier, and partner input used in managing these processes, as appropriate?

(5) How do you minimize overall costs associated with inspections, tests, and process or performance audits, as appropriate? How do you prevent defects and rework and minimize warranty costs, as appropriate?

(6) How do you improve your value creation processes to achieve better performance, to reduce variability, to improve products and services, and to keep the processes current with business needs and directions? How are improvements shared with other organizational units and processes?

6.1 Percent
Score

☑ **Approach**   ☑ **Deployment**   ☑ **Learning**   ☑ **Integration**

6.1a(1) How does your organization determine its key homeland security value creation processes (i.e., processes that are most critical to running and safeguarding your business) that enhance homeland security?

Interview notes:

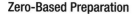

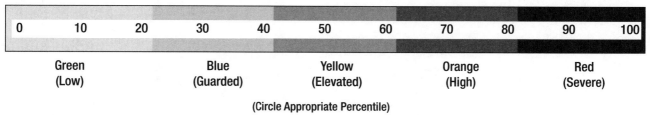

Zero-Based Preparation   **World-Class Preparation**

| 0 | 10 | 20 | 30 | 40 | 50 | 60 | 70 | 80 | 90 | 100 |

Green (Low)   Blue (Guarded)   Yellow (Elevated)   Orange (High)   Red (Severe)

(Circle Appropriate Percentile)

Zero-Based Organization	World-Class Organization
• Organization has no design of new programs and services for homeland security based on input regarding value-creation processes. • Organization has no process in place to ensure that homeland security programs and offerings are designed to reflect stakeholder input and focus on value-creation processes.	• Organization's surveys are used to determine key homeland security processes. Processes are flowcharted and designed to address the most critical security issues for the organization. • Employees at all levels are updated and asked to review all new initiatives to ensure that they address critical security issues and focus on key value creation processes for homeland security.

☑ **Approach**   ☑ **Deployment**   ☑ **Learning**   ☑ **Integration**

6.1a(1) Organization determines its key value creation processes that enhance homeland security.

+ Strengths

1.

2.

3.

– Opportunities for Improvement

1.

2.

3.

Homeland Security Planning Issues:

Short Term (1 to 2 years)

1.

2.

Long Term (2 years or more)

1.

2.

6.1a(2) How does your organization determine key value creation process requirements, incorporating customer, supplier, and partner input for critical homeland security processes?

Interview notes:

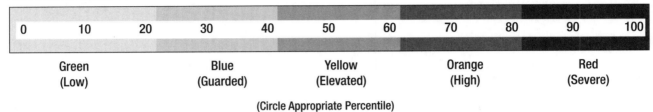

Zero-Based Preparation   **World-Class Preparation**

| 0 | 10 | 20 | 30 | 40 | 50 | 60 | 70 | 80 | 90 | 100 |

Green (Low)   Blue (Guarded)   Yellow (Elevated)   Orange (High)   Red (Severe)

(Circle Appropriate Percentile)

Zero-Based Organization

- Organization does not use a systematic approach to evaluate and improve key homeland security value creation processes.
- Organization does not include stakeholders to help determine key homeland security value creation processes.

World-Class Organization

- Organization has a structured evaluation process to ensure that key value creation processes for homeland security requirements are identified and flowcharted and involve all stakeholder groups.
- Organization incorporates a simple flowchart of key homeland security processes and includes key customers, suppliers, and partners to identify key value creation processes.

☑ Approach   ☑ Deployment   ☑ Learning   ☑ Integration

6.1a(2) Organization determines key value creation process requirements, incorporating customer, supplier, and partner input for critical homeland security processes.

+ Strengths

1.

2.

3.

– Opportunities for Improvement

1.

2.

3.

Homeland Security Planning Issues:

Short Term (1 to 2 years)

1.

2.

Long Term (2 years or more)

1.

2.

6.1a(3) How does your organization design critical homeland security processes to meet all key requirements?

Interview notes:

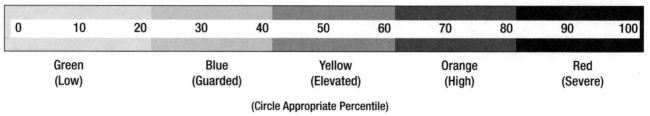

Zero-Based Preparation   **World-Class Preparation**

| 0 | 10 | 20 | 30 | 40 | 50 | 60 | 70 | 80 | 90 | 100 |

| Green | Blue | Yellow | Orange | Red |
| (Low) | (Guarded) | (Elevated) | (High) | (Severe) |

(Circle Appropriate Percentile)

Zero-Based Organization

- Organization has no quality control for homeland security processes that have been designed to ensure a safe work environment.
- Organization does not consider stakeholders and their requirements when designing key processes for homeland security.

World-Class Organization

- Organization conducts assessments to ensure that critical homeland security processes meet design requirements and incorporate cycle time and other efficiency and effectiveness factors into the design of the processes.
- Organization's homeland security program designs are reviewed by cross-functional employee and stakeholder teams to ensure that design requirements are being met.

☑ Approach   ☑ Deployment   ☑ Learning   ☑ Integration

6.1a(3) Organization designs critical homeland security processes to meet all key requirements.

+ Strengths
1.
2.
3.

– Opportunities for Improvement
1.
2.
3.

Homeland Security Planning Issues:

Short Term (1 to 2 years)
1.
2.

Long Term (2 years or more)
1.
2.

6.1a(4) How does your organization use key performance measures or indicators for critical homeland security processes to control and improve your value creation processes?

Interview notes:

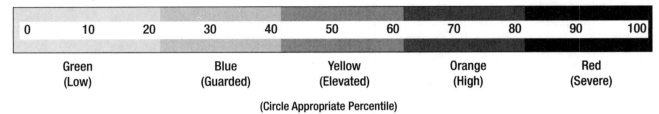

Zero-Based Preparation   World-Class Preparation

| 0 | 10 | 20 | 30 | 40 | 50 | 60 | 70 | 80 | 90 | 100 |

Green (Low)   Blue (Guarded)   Yellow (Elevated)   Orange (High)   Red (Severe)

(Circle Appropriate Percentile)

Zero-Based Organization

- Organization has no indicators in place to gauge out-of-control processes for key homeland security processes.
- Organization's value creation process design is not reviewed to determine if program and service offerings meet design requirements of homeland security for the organization.

World-Class Organization

- Organization has set up Service Quality Indicators (SQIs) for critical homeland security processes and uses them for control and improvement of its value creation processes.
- Organization has received input and agreement from key stakeholders when developing its performance measures for key homeland security processes. The indicators ensure that all key process requirements are met on a daily basis.

☑ Approach   ☑ Deployment   ☑ Learning   ☑ Integration

6.1a(4) Organization uses key performance measures or indicators for critical homeland security processes to control and improve value creation processes.

+ Strengths

1.
2.
3.

– Opportunities for Improvement

1.
2.
3.

Homeland Security Planning Issues:

Short Term (1 to 2 years)

1.
2.

Long Term (2 years or more)

1.
2.

6.1a(5) How does your organization minimize overall costs associated with homeland security inspections, tests, and process or performance audits?

Interview notes:

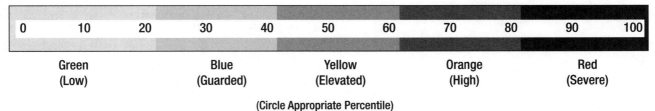

| 0 | 10 | 20 | 30 | 40 | 50 | 60 | 70 | 80 | 90 | 100 |

| Green
(Low) | | Blue
(Guarded) | | Yellow
(Elevated) | | Orange
(High) | | Red
(Severe) | |

(Circle Appropriate Percentile)

Zero-Based Organization

- Organization has no process in place to minimize overall costs associated with homeland security inspections, tests, and process or performance audits.

- Organization occasionally uses in-house self-assessment teams to conduct homeland security audits to minimize costs. Organization does not always consider costs when assessing homeland security initiatives.

World-Class Organization

- Organization uses in-house cross-functional employee teams to conduct homeland security inspections, tests, and process audits to minimize overall costs.

- Organization minimizes overall costs associated with conducting homeland security audits by using a self-assessment process that is conducted by outside stakeholder teams.

☑ Approach   ☑ Deployment   ☑ Learning   ☑ Integration

6.1a(5) Organization minimizes overall costs associated with homeland security inspections, tests, and process or performance audits.

+ Strengths

1.

2.

3.

– Opportunities for Improvement

1.

2.

3.

Homeland Security Planning Issues:

Short Term (1 to 2 years)

1.

2.

Long Term (2 years or more)

1.

2.

6.1a(6) How does your organization improve its value creation processes for homeland security to achieve better performance, to reduce variability, to improve product/service delivery, and to keep processes current with overall homeland security needs and directions?

Interview notes:

Zero-Based Preparation   **World-Class Preparation**

| 0 | 10 | 20 | 30 | 40 | 50 | 60 | 70 | 80 | 90 | 100 |

| Green | Blue | Yellow | Orange | Red |
| (Low) | (Guarded) | (Elevated) | (High) | (Severe) |

(Circle Appropriate Percentile)

Zero-Based Organization

- Organization does not have a systematic approach to evaluate and improve key homeland security processes within the organization.
- Organization does not evaluate its key homeland security initiatives to ensure better performance, to reduce variability, and to ensure overall effectiveness.

World-Class Organization

- Organization has a structured evaluation process to ensure that all value creation processes for homeland security meet design requirements, achieve better performance, and reduce variability.
- Organization conducts pilot tests on all key homeland security initiatives to ensure better performance, to reduce variability, and to improve all key processes.

☑ **Approach**   ☑ **Deployment**   ☑ **Learning**   ☑ **Integration**

6.1a(6) Organization improves value creation processes for homeland security to achieve better performance, to reduce variability, to improve product/service delivery, and to keep processes current with overall homeland security needs and directions.

+ Strengths

1.
2.
3.

– Opportunities for Improvement

1.
2.
3.

Homeland Security Planning Issues:

Short Term (1 to 2 years)

1.
2.

Long Term (2 years or more)

1.
2.

6.2 Support Processes (35 pts.)

Describe how your organization manages its key processes that support your value creation processes.

AREAS TO ADDRESS

a. **Support Processes**

(1) How does your organization determine its key support processes? What are your key processes for supporting your value creation processes?

(2) How do you determine key support process requirements, incorporating input from internal and external customers and from suppliers and partners, as appropriate? What are the key requirements for these processes?

(3) How do you design these processes to meet all the key requirements? How do you incorporate new technology and organizational knowledge into the design of these processes? How do you incorporate cycle time, productivity, cost control, and other efficiency and effectiveness factors into the design of the processes? How do you implement these processes to ensure they meet design requirements?

(4) What are your key performance measures or indicators used for the control and improvement of your support processes? How does your day-to-day operation of key support processes ensure meeting key performance requirements? How are in-process measures used in managing these processes? How is customer, supplier, and partner input used in managing these processes, as appropriate?

(5) How do you minimize overall costs associated with inspections, tests, and process or performance audits, as appropriate? How do you prevent defects and rework?

(6) How do you improve your support processes to achieve better performance, to reduce variability, and to keep the processes current with business needs and directions? How are improvements shared with other organizational units and processes?

6.2 Percent
Score

☑ Approach   ☑ Deployment   ☑ Learning   ☑ Integration

6.2a(1) How does your organization determine its key processes that support homeland security?

Interview notes:

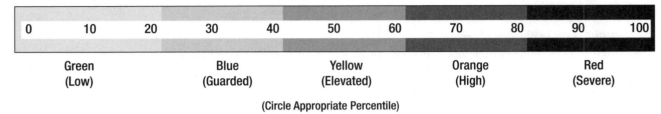

Zero-Based Preparation   **World-Class Preparation**

| 0 | 10 | 20 | 30 | 40 | 50 | 60 | 70 | 80 | 90 | 100 |

Green
(Low)

Blue
(Guarded)

Yellow
(Elevated)

Orange
(High)

Red
(Severe)

(Circle Appropriate Percentile)

Zero-Based Organization

- Organization does not seek input from stakeholders to determine key processes that support homeland security.
- Organization determines key processes that support homeland security without input from employees and stakeholder groups.

World-Class Organization

- Organization determines its critical processes that support homeland security initiatives based on focus group input from key stakeholder groups.
- Organization surveys employees, suppliers, customers, and partners annually to determine key processes that support homeland security.

☑ **Approach**   ☑ **Deployment**   ☑ **Learning**   ☑ **Integration**

6.2a(1) Organization determines its key processes that support homeland security.

+ Strengths

1.

2.

3.

– Opportunities for Improvement

1.

2.

3.

Homeland Security Planning Issues:

Short Term (1 to 2 years)

1.

2.

Long Term (2 years or more)

1.

2.

6.2a(2) How does your organization determine key support process requirements for homeland security, incorporating input from employees, suppliers, partners, and customers?

Interview notes:

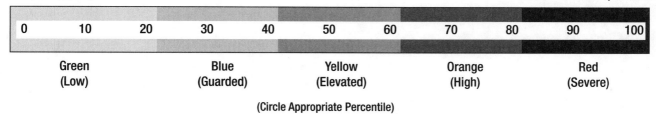

| Zero-Based Preparation | | | | World-Class Preparation |

| 0 | 10 | 20 | 30 | 40 | 50 | 60 | 70 | 80 | 90 | 100 |

| Green (Low) | Blue (Guarded) | Yellow (Elevated) | Orange (High) | Red (Severe) |

(Circle Appropriate Percentile)

Zero-Based Organization

- Organization has no formal design and implementation methodology to determine key support requirements for homeland security processes.
- Organization does not address key support requirements for homeland security processes.

World-Class Organization

- Organization determines key support process requirements for homeland security by using focus group data from key stakeholders.
- Organization's design and implementation plans for key support requirements for homeland security processes involve a cross-section of key stakeholders that make up a design team. The team provides input for the design, implementation, and evaluation.

☑ Approach   ☑ Deployment   ☑ Learning   ☑ Integration

6.2a(2) Organization determines key support process requirements for homeland security, incorporating input from employees, suppliers, partners, and customers.

+ Strengths

1.

2.

3.

– Opportunities for Improvement

1.

2.

3.

Homeland Security Planning Issues:

Short Term (1 to 2 years)

1.

2.

Long Term (2 years or more)

1.

2.

6.2a(3) How does your organization design support processes to meet all key homeland security process requirements?

Interview notes:

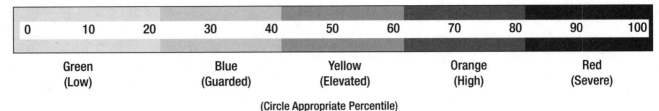

Zero-Based Preparation   **World-Class Preparation**

| 0 | 10 | 20 | 30 | 40 | 50 | 60 | 70 | 80 | 90 | 100 |

Green (Low)   Blue (Guarded)   Yellow (Elevated)   Orange (High)   Red (Severe)

(Circle Appropriate Percentile)

Zero-Based Organization

- Organization is not concerned with whether support processes meet key homeland security process requirements.
- Organization has no process in place to ensure that support processes meet key homeland security requirements.

World-Class Organization

- Organization conducts a formal assessment annually of key homeland security support processes to ensure that all design requirements are being met.
- Organization interviews a select number of key stakeholders quarterly to gauge the extent that support processes meet all homeland security requirements.

☑ Approach ☑ Deployment ☑ Learning ☑ Integration

6.2a(3) Organization designs support processes to meet all key homeland security process requirements.

+ Strengths
1.
2.
3.

– Opportunities for Improvement
1.
2.
3.

Homeland Security Planning Issues:

Short Term (1 to 2 years)
1.
2.

Long Term (2 years or more)
1.
2.

6.2a(4) How does your organization use key performance measures or indicators to control and improve your homeland security support processes?

Interview notes:

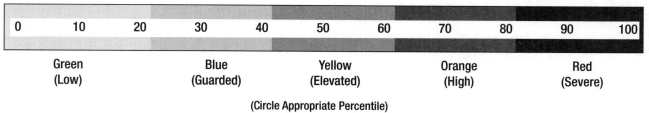

Zero-Based Preparation   **World-Class Preparation**

| 0 | 10 | 20 | 30 | 40 | 50 | 60 | 70 | 80 | 90 | 100 |

Green
(Low)

Blue
(Guarded)

Yellow
(Elevated)

Orange
(High)

Red
(Severe)

(Circle Appropriate Percentile)

Zero-Based Organization

- Organization has no key performance measures or indicators to control and/or improve homeland security support processes.
- Organization does not compare or benchmark other organizations' key performance measures or indicators for support processes to ensure the use of best practices.

World-Class Organization

- Organization has developed a security scoreboard to control and improve homeland security support processes.
- Organization conducts biannual assessments to measure the extent homeland security support processes are in control against the design of the process. Findings are used to improve the process.

☑ Approach   ☑ Deployment   ☑ Learning   ☑ Integration

6.2a(4) Organization uses key performance measures or indicators to control and improve homeland security support processes.

+ Strengths

1.

2.

3.

– Opportunities for Improvement

1.

2.

3.

Homeland Security Planning Issues:

Short Term (1 to 2 years)

1.

2.

Long Term (2 years or more)

1.

2.

6.2a(5) How does your organization minimize overall costs associated with inspections, tests, and homeland security support process audits?

Interview notes:

Zero-Based Preparation   **World-Class Preparation**

| 0 | 10 | 20 | 30 | 40 | 50 | 60 | 70 | 80 | 90 | 100 |

Green
(Low)

Blue
(Guarded)

Yellow
(Elevated)

Orange
(High)

Red
(Severe)

(Circle Appropriate Percentile)

Zero-Based Organization

- Organization has no process in place to minimize costs associated with inspections, tests, and homeland security support process audits.
- Organization never considers reviewing costs associated with homeland security support process audits.

World-Class Organization

- Organization has trained an internal audit team to conduct annual self-assessments of key homeland security support processes to minimize costs.
- Organization uses select employees and stakeholders to audit homeland security support processes to save inspection costs.

✔ Approach   ✔ Deployment   ✔ Learning   ✔ Integration

6.2a(5) Organization minimizes overall cost associated with inspections, tests, and homeland security support process audits.

+ Strengths

1.
2.
3.

– Opportunities for Improvement

1.
2.
3.

Homeland Security Planning Issues:

Short Term (1 to 2 years)

1.
2.

Long Term (2 years or more)

1.
2.

6.2a(6) How does your organization improve homeland security support processes to achieve better performance, reduce variability, and keep processes current with overall homeland security needs and directions?

Interview notes:

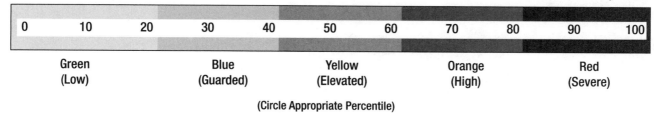

Zero-Based Preparation   **World-Class Preparation**

| 0 | 10 | 20 | 30 | 40 | 50 | 60 | 70 | 80 | 90 | 100 |

| Green | Blue | Yellow | Orange | Red |
| (Low) | (Guarded) | (Elevated) | (High) | (Severe) |

(Circle Appropriate Percentile)

Zero-Based Organization

- Organization does not consistently review key homeland security support processes to reduce variability and to keep them current with homeland security goals and plans.
- Organization has no concern for improving key homeland security support processes.

World-Class Organization

- Organization achieves better performance and reduces variability by documenting best practices of all key homeland security support processes and assigning cycle times.
- Organization conducts analysis of key homeland security support processes and reengineers the processes after benchmarking best practices to ensure reduced variability and to keep current with the organization's goals and plans.

☑ **Approach**   ☑ **Deployment**   ☑ **Learning**   ☑ **Integration**

6.2a(6) Organization improves homeland security support processes to achieve better performance, reduce variability, and keep processes current with overall homeland security needs and directions.

+ Strengths

1.
2.
3.

– Opportunities for Improvement

1.
2.
3.

Homeland Security Planning Issues:

Short Term (1 to 2 years)

1.
2.

Long Term (2 years or more)

1.
2.

Notes

9 Category 7 Business Results

7 Business Results (450 pts.)[16]

The Business Results Category examines your organization's performance and improvement in key homeland security areas—customer satisfaction, product and service performance, financial and marketplace performance, human resource results, operational performance, and governance and social responsibility. Also examined are performance levels of homeland security initiatives relative to those of competitors.

 Forms can be downloaded from the CD-ROM located inside the back cover of this book.

7.1 Customer-Focused Results (75 pts.)

Summarize your organization's key customer-focused results, including customer satisfaction and customer-perceived value. Segment your results by customer groups and market segments, as appropriate. Include appropriate comparative data.

AREAS TO ADDRESS

a. Customer-Focused Results

    (1) What are your current levels and trends in key measures or indicators of customer satisfaction and dissatisfaction? How do these compare with competitors' levels of customer satisfaction?

    (2) What are your current levels and trends in key measures or indicators of customer-perceived value, including customer loyalty and retention, positive referral, and other aspects of building relationships with customers, as appropriate?

7.1 Percent
Score

✔ Performance Levels   ✔ Trends   ✔ Comparisons   ✔ Linkage   ✔ Gap

7.1a(1) What are your organization's current levels and trends in customer satisfaction and dissatisfaction with your organization's homeland security initiatives?

Interview notes:

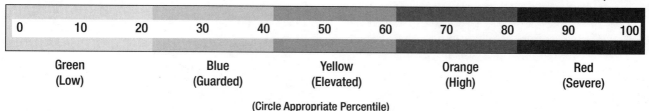

Zero-Based Preparation   **World-Class Preparation**

| 0 | 10 | 20 | 30 | 40 | 50 | 60 | 70 | 80 | 90 | 100 |

Green (Low)   Blue (Guarded)   Yellow (Elevated)   Orange (High)   Red (Severe)

(Circle Appropriate Percentile)

Zero-Based Organization

- Organization does not trend customer satisfaction and dissatisfaction data to gauge customer concerns regarding the organization's homeland security initiatives.
- Organization does not collect satisfaction/dissatisfaction data from customers regarding homeland security issues.

World-Class Organization

- Organization collects and trends satisfaction and dissatisfaction data to gauge its customers' ongoing satisfaction with homeland security initiatives that involve customers and customer groups.
- Organization uses customer satisfaction/dissatisfaction trend data to improve its homeland security initiatives that involve customers.

☑ Performance Levels   ☑ Trends   ☑ Comparisons   ☑ Linkage   ☑ Gap

7.1a(1) Organization's current levels and trends of customer satisfaction and dissatisfaction with its homeland security initiatives.

+ Strengths

1.
2.
3.

– Opportunities for Improvement

1.
2.
3.

Homeland Security Planning Issues:

Short Term (1 to 2 years)

1.
2.

Long Term (2 years or more)

1.
2.

7.1a(2) What are your organization's current levels and trends of customer-perceived value with organization's homeland security initiatives (i.e., customer loyalty and retention, positive referral, and other aspects of building relationships with customers)?

Interview notes:

Zero-Based Preparation   **World-Class Preparation**

| 0 | 10 | 20 | 30 | 40 | 50 | 60 | 70 | 80 | 90 | 100 |

| Green
(Low) | Blue
(Guarded) | Yellow
(Elevated) | Orange
(High) | Red
(Severe) |

(Circle Appropriate Percentile)

Zero-Based Organization

- Organization does not collect data to gauge its customers' perceived value of homeland security initiatives.
- Organization has no concern for gauging customer-perceived value regarding homeland security initiatives that are mandated for security.

World-Class Organization

- Organization aggregates trend data of customer perception of the effectiveness of homeland security initiatives that are incorporated into its product/service delivery.
- Organization collects current levels and trend data of customer satisfaction/dissatisfaction with homeland security initiatives, based on customer loyalty and retention, and positive referrals.

☑ Performance Levels   ☑ Trends   ☑ Comparisons   ☑ Linkage   ☑ Gap

7.1a(2) Organization's current levels and trends of customer-perceived value with its homeland security initiatives.

+ Strengths
1.
2.
3.

– Opportunities for Improvement
1.
2.
3.

Homeland Security Planning Issues:

Short Term (1 to 2 years)
1.
2.

Long Term (2 years or more)
1.
2.

7.2 Product and Service Results (75 pts.)

Summarize your organization's key product and service performance results. Segment your results by product groups, customer groups, and market segments, as appropriate. Include appropriate comparative data.

AREA TO ADDRESS

a. **Product and Service Results**

What are your current levels and trends in key measures or indicators of product and service performance that are important to your customers? How do these results compare with your competitors' performance?

7.2 Percent
Score

✔ Performance Levels   ✔ Trends   ✔ Comparisons   ✔ Linkage   ✔ Gap

7.2a What are your organization's current levels and trends of product and service performance safeguarded by the organization's homeland security initiatives that are considered important to customers?

Interview notes:

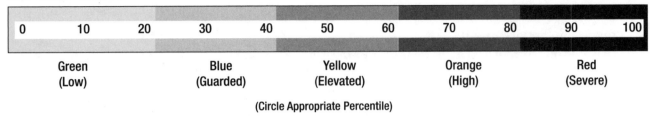

| Zero-Based Preparation | | | | World-Class Preparation |

| 0 | 10 | 20 | 30 | 40 | 50 | 60 | 70 | 80 | 90 | 100 |

| Green (Low) | Blue (Guarded) | Yellow (Elevated) | Orange (High) | Red (Severe) |

(Circle Appropriate Percentile)

Zero-Based Organization

- Organization collects trend data for customer product/service delivery only during times of high and severe security alerts.
- Organization does not consistently collect current level and trend data on product/service performance that is safeguarded by its homeland security initiatives.

World-Class Organization

- Organization has positive two-year trends for customer product and service performance delivery that are safeguarded by its homeland security initiatives.
- Organization has a three-year positive trend in reducing cycle time for customer product/service checks, based on its homeland security initiatives.

✔ Performance Levels   ✔ Trends   ✔ Comparisons   ✔ Linkage   ✔ Gap

7.2a Organization's current levels and trends of product and service performance safeguarded by its homeland security initiatives that are considered important to customers.

+ Strengths

1.

2.

3.

– Opportunities for Improvement

1.

2.

3.

Homeland Security Planning Issues:

Short Term (1 to 2 years)

1.

2.

Long Term (2 years or more)

1.

2.

7.3 Financial and Market Results (75 pts.)

Summarize your organization's key financial and marketplace performance results by market segments, as appropriate. Include appropriate comparative data.

AREAS TO ADDRESS

a. **Financial and Market Results**

(1) What are your current levels and trends in key measures or indicators of financial performance, including aggregate measures of financial return and economic value, as appropriate?

(2) What are your current levels and trends in key measures or indicators of marketplace performance, including market share or position, business growth, and new markets entered, as appropriate?

7.3 Percent Score

 Performance Levels   Trends   ✔ Comparisons   ✔ Linkage   Gap

7.3a(1) What are your organization's current levels and trends of financial performance that involve homeland security initiatives?

Interview notes:

Zero-Based Preparation   **World-Class Preparation**

0	10	20	30	40	50	60	70	80	90	100

Green (Low)	Blue (Guarded)	Yellow (Elevated)	Orange (High)	Red (Severe)

(Circle Appropriate Percentile)

Zero-Based Organization

- Organization has not identified a set of key budgetary and financial measures to gauge overall impact of homeland security initiatives. Many of the measures are inconsistent and anecdotal.

- Organization does not collect trend data on financial performance regarding homeland security initiatives.

World-Class Organization

- Organization tracks current levels and trends of financial and market performance to gauge overall effectiveness and impact of homeland security initiatives.

- Organization tracks and trends homeland security expenditures per employee, partner, supplier, and customer. The measures are used to gauge their economic impact against the organization's strategic plans and goals.

☑ Performance Levels   ☑ Trends   ☑ Comparisons   ☑ Linkage   ☑ Gap

7.3a(1) Organization's current levels and trends of financial performance that involve homeland security initiatives.

+ Strengths
1.
2.
3.

– Opportunities for Improvement
1.
2.
3.

Homeland Security Planning Issues:

Short Term (1 to 2 years)
1.
2.

Long Term (2 years or more)
1.
2.

7.3a(2) What are your organization's current levels and trends of marketplace performance that involve homeland security initiatives?

Interview notes:

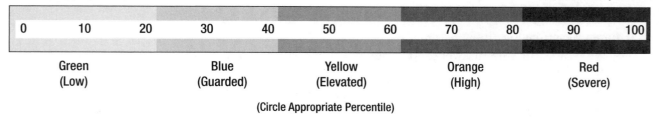

Zero-Based Preparation   **World-Class Preparation**

| 0 | 10 | 20 | 30 | 40 | 50 | 60 | 70 | 80 | 90 | 100 |

| Green
(Low) | Blue
(Guarded) | Yellow
(Elevated) | Orange
(High) | Red
(Severe) |

(Circle Appropriate Percentile)

Zero-Based Organization

- Organization has not collected data to gauge its marketplace performance involving homeland security initiatives that have been implemented for its key customers over the past two years.
- Organization has not holistically reviewed or collected marketplace performance data that involves its homeland security initiatives.

World-Class Organization

- Organization has a positive three-year trend regarding marketplace performance that involves homeland security initiatives.
- Organization has had positive trends in the market based on its homeland security initiatives with both key customers and suppliers.

☑ **Performance Levels**   ☑ **Trends**   ☑ **Comparisons**   ☑ **Linkage**   ☑ **Gap**

7.3a(2) Organization's current levels and trends of marketplace performance that involve homeland security initiatives.

+ Strengths

1.

2.

3.

– Opportunities for Improvement

1.

2.

3.

Homeland Security Planning Issues:

Short Term (1 to 2 years)

1.

2.

Long Term (2 years or more)

1.

2.

7.4 Human Resource Results (75 pts.)

Summarize your organization's key human resource results, including work system performance and employee learning, development, well-being, and satisfaction. Segment your results to address the diversity of your workforce and the different types and categories of employees, as appropriate. Include appropriate comparative data.

AREAS TO ADDRESS

a. **Human Resource Results**

   (1) What are your current levels and trends in key measures or indicators of work system performance and effectiveness?

   (2) What are your current levels and trends in key measures of employee learning and development?

   (3) What are your current levels and trends in key measures or indicators of employee well-being, satisfaction, and dissatisfaction?

7.4 Percent
Score

 Performance Levels   Trends   Comparisons   Linkage   Gap

7.4a(1) What are your organization's current levels and trends of work system performance and effectiveness that involve homeland security initiatives?

Interview notes:

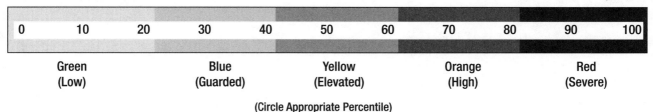

Zero-Based Preparation					World-Class Preparation

0   10   20   30   40   50   60   70   80   90   100

Green (Low)	Blue (Guarded)	Yellow (Elevated)	Orange (High)	Red (Severe)

(Circle Appropriate Percentile)

Zero-Based Organization

- Organization does not measure and trend results of work system performance that involve homeland security initiatives.
- Organization uses only limited measures to gauge work system performance that involves homeland security initiatives.

World-Class Organization

- Organization measures and trends data that gauge its work system performance and effectiveness that are impacted by homeland security initiatives.
- Organization tracks and trends work layout improvement and job rotation in areas that involve homeland security initiatives.

☑ Performance Levels   ☑ Trends   ☑ Comparisons   ☑ Linkage   ☑ Gap

7.4a(1) Organization's current levels and trends of work system performance and effectiveness that involve homeland security initiatives.

+ Strengths

1.
2.
3.

– Opportunities for Improvement

1.
2.
3.

Homeland Security Planning Issues:

Short Term (1 to 2 years)

1.
2.

Long Term (2 years or more)

1.
2.

7.4a(2) What are your organization's current levels and trends of employee learning and development that involve homeland security initiatives?

Interview notes:

Zero-Based Preparation    **World-Class Preparation**

| 0 | 10 | 20 | 30 | 40 | 50 | 60 | 70 | 80 | 90 | 100 |

| Green
(Low) | Blue
(Guarded) | Yellow
(Elevated) | Orange
(High) | Red
(Severe) |

(Circle Appropriate Percentile)

Zero-Based Organization

- Organization collects limited data on employee learning and development that involves homeland security initiatives.
- Organization collects data on training that involves homeland security issues, but never uses trend results to gauge progress.

World-Class Organization

- Organization has a three-year positive trend of employee learning and development that involves homeland security initiatives.
- Organization has experienced a 40% increase over three years in the number of employees who have been trained on homeland security issues.

☑ Performance Levels ☑ Trends ☑ Comparisons ☑ Linkage ☑ Gap

7.4a(2) Organization's current levels and trends of employee learning and development involving homeland security initiatives.

+ Strengths
1.
2.
3.

– Opportunities for Improvement
1.
2.
3.

Homeland Security Planning Issues:

Short Term (1 to 2 years)
1.
2.

Long Term (2 years or more)
1.
2.

7.4a(3) What are your organization's current levels and trends of employee well-being, satisfaction, and dissatisfaction that involve the organization's homeland security initiatives?

Interview notes:

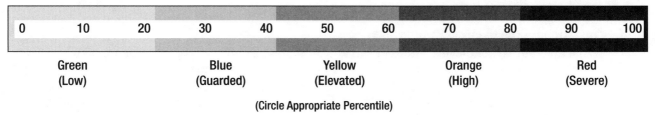

Zero-Based Preparation   **World-Class Preparation**

| 0 | 10 | 20 | 30 | 40 | 50 | 60 | 70 | 80 | 90 | 100 |

Green	Blue	Yellow	Orange	Red
(Low)	(Guarded)	(Elevated)	(High)	(Severe)

(Circle Appropriate Percentile)

Zero-Based Organization

- Organization does not gauge employee well-being, satisfaction, and dissatisfaction with its homeland security initiatives.
- Organization collects employee satisfaction data but does not collect satisfaction data related to employee satisfaction with homeland security initiatives.

World-Class Organization

- Organization collects and trends data on employee well-being, satisfaction, and dissatisfaction with homeland security initiatives.
- Organization has collected and trended over three years of employee satisfaction results that involve homeland security issues and initiatives.

☑ Performance Levels   ☑ Trends   ☑ Comparisons   ☑ Linkage   ☑ Gap

7.4a(3) Organization's current levels and trends of employee well-being, satisfaction, and dissatisfaction involving homeland security initiatives.

+ Strengths

1.
2.
3.

– Opportunities for Improvement

1.
2.
3.

Homeland Security Planning Issues:

Short Term (1 to 2 years)

1.
2.

Long Term (2 years or more)

1.
2.

7.5 Organizational Effectiveness Results (75 pts.)

Summarize your organization's key operational performance results that contribute to the achievement of organizational effectiveness. Segment your results by product groups and market segments, as appropriate. Include appropriate comparative data.

AREAS TO ADDRESS

a. **Organizational Effectiveness Results**

(1) What are your current levels and trends in key measures or indicators of the operational performance of your key value creation processes? Include productivity, cycle time, supplier and partner performance, and other appropriate measures of effectiveness and efficiency.

(2) What are your current levels and trends in key measures or indicators of the operational performance of your key support processes? Include productivity, cycle time, supplier and partner performance, and other appropriate measures of effectiveness and efficiency.

(3) What are your results for key measures or indicators of accomplishment of organizational strategy and action plans?

7.5 Percent
Score

✔ Performance Levels   ✔ Trends   ✔ Comparisons   ✔ Linkage   ✔ Gap

7.5a(1) What are your organization's current levels and trends of the operational performance of your key value creation processes for homeland security?

Interview notes:

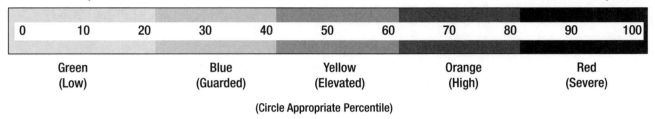

Zero-Based Preparation   **World-Class Preparation**

| 0 | 10 | 20 | 30 | 40 | 50 | 60 | 70 | 80 | 90 | 100 |

Green (Low)   Blue (Guarded)   Yellow (Elevated)   Orange (High)   Red (Severe)

(Circle Appropriate Percentile)

Zero-Based Organization

- Organization does not consistently collect key performance results for operational performance of key value creation processes for homeland security.
- Organization's measures for key operational results of homeland security processes appear limited.

World-Class Organization

- Organization shows positive levels and trends regarding key value creation processes for homeland security by using a productivity index known as Service Quality Indicators (SQIs).
- Organization's value creation processes for homeland security are identified, tracked, and trended to support workplace safety.

☑ Performance Levels ☑ Trends ☑ Comparisons ☑ Linkage ☑ Gap

7.5a(1) Organization's current levels and trends of the operational performance of key value creation processes for homeland security.

+ Strengths
1.
2.
3.

– Opportunities for Improvement
1.
2.
3.

Homeland Security Planning Issues:

Short Term (1 to 2 years)
1.
2.

Long Term (2 years or more)
1.
2.

7.5a(2) What are your organization's current levels and trends of operational performance of key support processes for homeland security?

Interview notes:

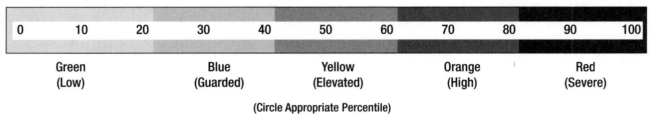

Zero-Based Preparation   **World-Class Preparation**

| 0 | 10 | 20 | 30 | 40 | 50 | 60 | 70 | 80 | 90 | 100 |

| Green | Blue | Yellow | Orange | Red |
| (Low) | (Guarded) | (Elevated) | (High) | (Severe) |

(Circle Appropriate Percentile)

Zero-Based Organization

- Organization does not collect trend data on operational performance of key support processes for homeland security.
- Organization's trend data collected for operational performance of key support processes for homeland security has had a steady decrease of 50% over three years.

World-Class Organization

- Organization's levels and trends of operational performance of key support processes for homeland security have four-year positive trends.
- Organization's key measures of key support processes for homeland security support the organization's goals and objectives for workplace safety with three-year positive trends.

☑ Performance Levels   ☑ Trends   ☑ Comparisons   ☑ Linkage   ☑ Gap

7.5a(2) Organization's current levels and tends of operational performance of key support processes for homeland security.

+ Strengths

1.

2.

3.

– Opportunities for Improvement

1.

2.

3.

Homeland Security Planning Issues:

Short Term (1 to 2 years)

1.

2.

Long Term (2 years or more)

1.

2.

7.5a(3) What are your organization's results for accomplishment of organizational strategy and action plans that involve homeland security initiatives?

Interview notes:

Zero-Based Preparation   **World-Class Preparation**

0	10	20	30	40	50	60	70	80	90	100

Green	Blue	Yellow	Orange	Red
(Low)	(Guarded)	(Elevated)	(High)	(Severe)

(Circle Appropriate Percentile)

Zero-Based Organization

- Organization does not collect results data for accomplishment of its strategies and action plans for homeland security initiatives.

- Organization has no consistent method for collecting data and measuring results for accomplishment of strategies and action plans that involve homeland security initiatives.

World-Class Organization

- Organization has accomplished 92% of the strategies and action plans that involve homeland security initiatives.

- Organization collects results data on completion of strategies and action plans that involve homeland security initiatives. The organization has experienced a 98% accomplishment rate.

☑ Performance Levels   ☑ Trends   ☑ Comparisons   ☑ Linkage   ☑ Gap

7.5a(3) Organization's results for accomplishment of organizational strategy and action plans that involve homeland security initiatives.

+ Strengths

1.

2.

3.

– Opportunities for Improvement

1.

2.

3.

Homeland Security Planning Issues:

Short Term (1 to 2 years)

1.

2.

Long Term (2 years or more)

1.

2.

7.6 Governance and Social Responsibility Results (75 pts.)

Summarize your organization's key governance and social responsibility results, including evidence of fiscal accountability, ethical behavior, legal compliance, and organizational citizenship. Segment your results by business units, as appropriate. Include appropriate comparative data.

AREAS TO ADDRESS

a. Governance and Social Responsibility Results

(1) What are your key current findings and trends in key measures of indicators of fiscal accountability, both internal and external, as appropriate?

(2) What are your results for key measures or indicators of ethical behavior and of stakeholder trust in the governance of your organization?

(3) What are your results for key measures or indicators of regulatory and legal compliance?

(4) What are your results for key measures or indicators of organizational citizenship in support of your key communities?

7.6 Percent Score

 Performance Levels   Trends   Comparisons   ☑ Linkage   ☑ Gap

7.6a(1) What are your organization's key current findings and trends of fiscal accountability for homeland security initiatives?

Interview notes:

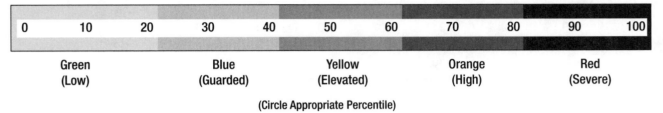

Zero-Based Preparation				World-Class Preparation

0   10   20   30   40   50   60   70   80   90   100

Green (Low)	Blue (Guarded)	Yellow (Elevated)	Orange (High)	Red (Severe)

(Circle Appropriate Percentile)

Zero-Based Organization

- Organization does not collect consistent data regarding fiscal accountability for homeland security initiatives.
- Organization collects limited data and trends for fiscal accountability for homeland security initiatives.

World-Class Organization

- Organization's findings and trends for fiscal accountability for homeland security initiatives show a positive three-year trend.
- Organization shows a positive four-year trend regarding fiscal accountability for homeland security initiatives. Data are used to identify additional risk factors and to address auditor recommendations.

☑ Performance Levels   ☑ Trends   ☑ Comparisons   ☑ Linkage   ☑ Gap

7.6a(1) Organization's key current findings and trends of fiscal accountability for homeland security initiatives.

+ Strengths

1.

2.

3.

– Opportunities for Improvement

1.

2.

3.

Homeland Security Planning Issues:

Short Term (1 to 2 years)

1.

2.

Long Term (2 years or more)

1.

2.

7.6a(2) What are your organization's key measures of ethical behavior and stakeholder trust regarding homeland security initiatives?

Interview notes:

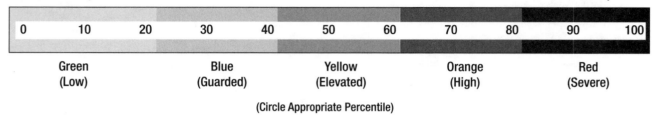

Zero-Based Preparation   **World-Class Preparation**

| 0 | 10 | 20 | 30 | 40 | 50 | 60 | 70 | 80 | 90 | 100 |

| Green | Blue | Yellow | Orange | Red |
| (Low) | (Guarded) | (Elevated) | (High) | (Severe) |

(Circle Appropriate Percentile)

Zero-Based Organization

- Organization does not have measures in place to gauge ethical behavior and stakeholder trust regarding homeland security policies and procedures.
- Organization collects no data on ethical behavior and stakeholder trust regarding homeland security issues and initiatives.

World-Class Organization

- Organization measures employees, customers, partners, and suppliers against a documented ethical code of standards for homeland security.
- Organization ensures that all employees, partners, suppliers, and customers go through a periodic ethics audit regarding adherence to the organization's homeland security policies and procedures.

☑ Performance Levels   ☑ Trends   ☑ Comparisons   ☑ Linkage   ☑ Gap

7.6a(2) Organization's key measures of ethical behavior and stakeholder trust regarding homeland security initiatives.

+ Strengths
1.
2.
3.

– Opportunities for Improvement
1.
2.
3.

Homeland Security Planning Issues:

Short Term (1 to 2 years)
1.
2.

Long Term (2 years or more)
1.
2.

7.6a(3) What are your organization's results for regulatory and legal compliance that involve homeland security initiatives?

Interview notes:

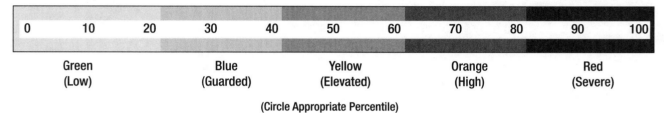

Zero-Based Preparation   **World-Class Preparation**

| 0 | 10 | 20 | 30 | 40 | 50 | 60 | 70 | 80 | 90 | 100 |

| Green | Blue | Yellow | Orange | Red |
| (Low) | (Guarded) | (Elevated) | (High) | (Severe) |

(Circle Appropriate Percentile)

Zero-Based Organization

- Organization does not consistently collect regulatory and legal compliance data for homeland security issues.
- Organization collects limited regulatory and legal homeland security compliance results outside of what is mandated by state and federal agencies.

World-Class Organization

- Organization collects data and trends results over three years for regulatory and legal compliance issues that involve homeland security issues.
- Organization collects and trends data on homeland security regulatory and legal compliance issues and uses results to improve compliance throughout the organization.

✔ Performance Levels   ✔ Trends   ✔ Comparisons   ✔ Linkage   ✔ Gap

7.6a(3) Organization's results for regulatory and legal compliance that involve homeland security initiatives.

+ Strengths

1.

2.

3.

– Opportunities for Improvement

1.

2.

3.

Homeland Security Planning Issues:

Short Term (1 to 2 years)

1.

2.

Long Term (2 years or more)

1.

2.

7.6a(4) What are your organization's results for support of its key communities homeland security efforts?

Interview notes:

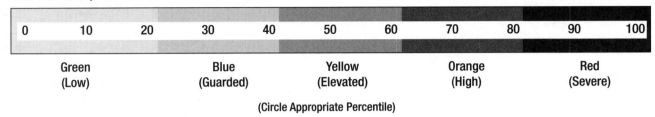

Zero-Based Preparation   **World-Class Preparation**

| 0 | 10 | 20 | 30 | 40 | 50 | 60 | 70 | 80 | 90 | 100 |

Green (Low)   Blue (Guarded)   Yellow (Elevated)   Orange (High)   Red (Severe)

(Circle Appropriate Percentile)

Zero-Based Organization

- Organization does not collect and trend homeland security results that support communities in which the organization is located.
- Organization never considers collecting and trending key indicators that support a community's homeland security efforts and initiatives.

World-Class Organization

- Organization collects and trends homeland security results that support communities where the organization is located.
- Organization aligns and compares its homeland security trends and results with community results to support an integrated effort that supports homeland security community-wide.

✔ Performance Levels   ✔ Trends   ✔ Comparisons   ✔ Linkage   ✔ Gap

7.6a(4) Organization's results for support of its key communities homeland security efforts.

+ Strengths

1.
2.
3.

– Opportunities for Improvement

1.
2.
3.

Homeland Security Planning Issues:

Short Term (1 to 2 years)

1.
2.

Long Term (2 years or more)

1.
2.

Notes

Summary of Assessment Items for Homeland Security
(Based on Baldrige Criteria)
Transfer all assessment item percent scores from the category worksheets.

SUMMARY OF ASSESSMENT ITEMS	Total Points Possible	Percent Score 0–100% (10%units)	Score (A + B)
	A	B	C
1 Leadership			
1.1 Organizational Leadership	70	_____%	
1.2 Social Responsibility	50	_____%	
CATEGORY TOTAL	120		_____
			(Sum C)
2 Strategic Planning			
2.1 Strategy Development	40	_____%	_____
2.2 Strategy Deployment	45	_____%	_____
CATEGORY TOTAL	85		_____
			(Sum C)
3 Customer and Market Focus			
3.1 Customer and Market Knowledge	40	_____%	_____
3.2 Customer Relationships and Satisfaction	45	_____%	_____
CATEGORY TOTAL	85		_____
			(Sum C)
4 Measurement, Analysis, and Knowledge Management			
4.1 Measurement and Analysis of Organizational Performance	45	_____%	_____
4.2 Information and Knowledge Management	45	_____%	_____
CATEGORY TOTAL	90		_____
			(Sum C)

Continued

Continued

SUMMARY OF ASSESSMENT ITEMS	Total Points Possible A	Score 0–100% (10%units) B	Score (A + B) C
5 Human Resource Focus			
5.1 Work Systems	35	_____%	
5.2 Employee Learning and Motivation	25	_____%	
5.3 Employee Well-Being and Satisfaction	25	_____%	
CATEGORY TOTAL	85		_____
			(Sum C)
6 Process Management			
6.1 Value Creation Processes	50	_____%	_____
6.2 Support Processes	35	_____%	_____
CATEGORY TOTAL	85		_____
			(Sum C)
7 Business Results			
7.1 Customer-Focused Results	75	_____%	_____
7.2 Product and Service Results	75	_____%	_____
7.3 Financial and Market Results	75	_____%	_____
7.4 Human Resource Results	75	_____%	_____
7.5 Organizational Effectiveness Results	75	_____%	_____
7.6 Governance and Social Responsibility Results	75	_____%	_____
CATEGORY TOTAL	450		_____
			(Sum C)
TOTAL POINTS	1000		_____

Hierarchy of Homeland Security Assessment Needs
(Based on Baldrige Criteria)

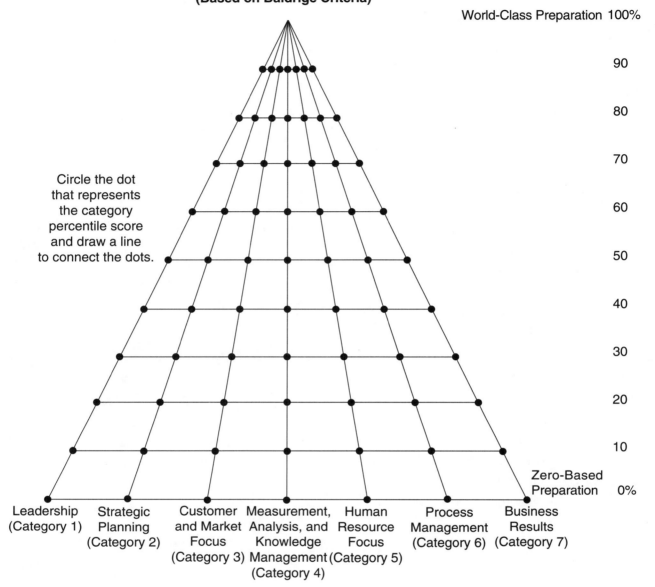

10 Transforming Assessment Findings into Actionable Strategies for a Homeland Security Plan

The assessment of the organization is complete. Now the next step is to transform the assessment results into actionable short- and long-term strategies for a homeland security plan.

The assessment team should begin this process by reviewing strengths and opportunities for improvement within the areas assessed. The assessment team members will need to reach a consensus on short- and long-term strategic issues for each area. After this process is complete, the team should go back through the assessment manual and collect item percentage scores. The assessment percentages should be shaded within each appropriate item bar graph. Illustrations are given to help the team complete both the assessment bar graphs and strategic planning worksheets.

 Forms can be downloaded from the CD-ROM located inside the back cover of this book.

ORGANIZATIONAL ASSESSMENT BAR GRAPH
(Shade in assessment percentages on bar graphs from
item score boxes located throughout workbook.)

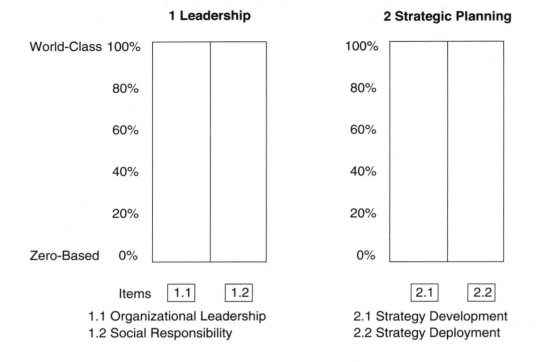

1 Leadership

World-Class 100%

80%

60%

40%

20%

Zero-Based 0%

Items 1.1 1.2

1.1 Organizational Leadership
1.2 Social Responsibility

2 Strategic Planning

100%

80%

60%

40%

20%

0%

2.1 2.2

2.1 Strategy Development
2.2 Strategy Deployment

Note: Based on bar graphs, select and prioritize within each category short- and long-term strategic issues identified in the assessment and list below.

1 Leadership
Category

Priority 1 _____ Short term

_____ Long term

Priority 2 _____ Short term

_____ Long term

Priority 3 _____ Short term

_____ Long term

2 Strategic Planning
Category

Priority 1 _____ Short term

_____ Long term

Priority 2 _____ Short term

_____ Long term

Priority 3 _____ Short term

_____ Long term

ORGANIZATIONAL ASSESSMENT BAR GRAPH
(Shade in assessment percentages on bar graphs from
item score boxes located throughout workbook.)

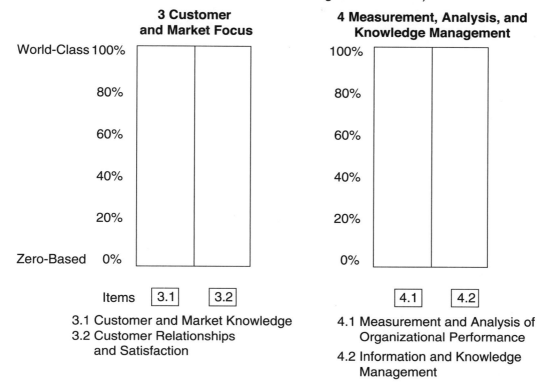

**3 Customer
and Market Focus**

World-Class 100%

80%

60%

40%

20%

Zero-Based   0%

Items 3.1   3.2

3.1 Customer and Market Knowledge
3.2 Customer Relationships
and Satisfaction

**4 Measurement, Analysis, and
Knowledge Management**

100%

80%

60%

40%

20%

0%

4.1   4.2

4.1 Measurement and Analysis of
Organizational Performance
4.2 Information and Knowledge
Management

Note: Based on bar graphs, select and prioritize within each category short- and
long-term strategic issues identified in the assessment and list below.

**3 Customer and Market Focus
Category**

Priority 1 _____ Short term

_____ Long term

Priority 2 _____ Short term

_____ Long term

Priority 3 _____ Short term

_____ Long term

**4 Measurement, Analysis, and
Knowledge Management Category**

Priority 1 _____ Short term

_____ Long term

Priority 2 _____ Short term

_____ Long term

Priority 3 _____ Short term

_____ Long term

ORGANIZATIONAL ASSESSMENT BAR GRAPH
(Shade in assessment percentages on bar graphs from
item score boxes located throughout workbook.)

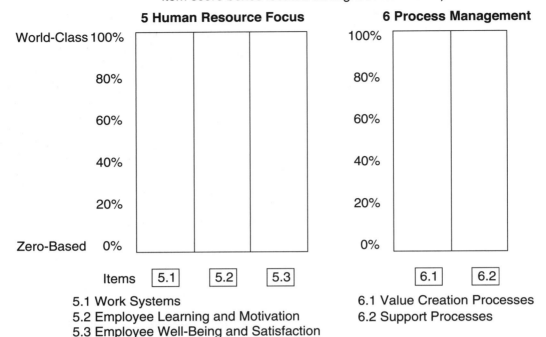

5 Human Resource Focus

World-Class 100%

80%

60%

40%

20%

Zero-Based 0%

Items 5.1 5.2 5.3

5.1 Work Systems
5.2 Employee Learning and Motivation
5.3 Employee Well-Being and Satisfaction

6 Process Management

100%

80%

60%

40%

20%

0%

6.1 6.2

6.1 Value Creation Processes
6.2 Support Processes

Note: Based on bar graphs, select and prioritize within each category short- and
long-term strategic issues identified in the assessment and list below.

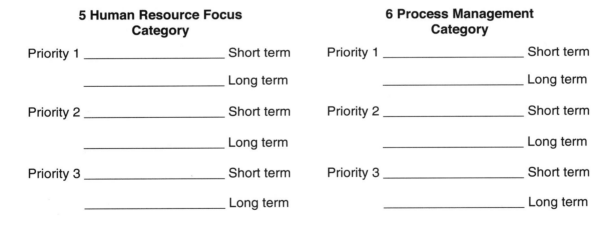

**5 Human Resource Focus
Category**

Priority 1 _____ Short term

_____ Long term

Priority 2 _____ Short term

_____ Long term

Priority 3 _____ Short term

_____ Long term

**6 Process Management
Category**

Priority 1 _____ Short term

_____ Long term

Priority 2 _____ Short term

_____ Long term

Priority 3 _____ Short term

_____ Long term

ORGANIZATIONAL ASSESSMENT BAR GRAPH
(Shade in assessment percentages on bar graphs from
item score boxes located throughout workbook.)

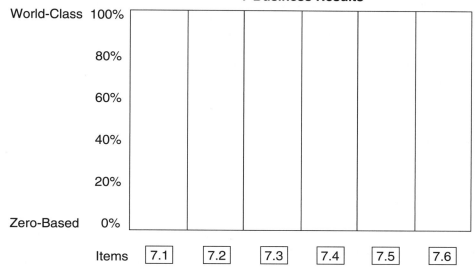

7 Business Results

7.1 Customer-Focused Results
7.2 Product and Service Results
7.3 Financial and Market Results
7.4 Human Resource Results
7.5 Organizational Effectiveness Results
7.6 Governance and Social Responsibility Results

Note: Based on bar graphs, select and prioritize within each category short- and long-term strategic issues identified in the assessment and list below.

7 Business Results Category

Priority 1 _____ Short term

_____ Long term

Priority 2 _____ Short term

_____ Long term

Priority 3 _____ Short term

_____ Long term

The shaded bar graphs will help the assessment team identify specific items within each category of the organization that need improvement as homeland security issues.

The next step for the team after all scores have been shaded in on the bar graphs is to select and prioritize short- and long-term strategic planning issues within each category that were previously identified through the assessment process by the team. The team will go through the process of prioritizing the strategic short- and long-term planning issues within each category that need to be developed into actionable improvement strategies for the organization.

After identifying and prioritizing strategic planning issues within all seven Baldrige Categories, the team should select the top three short- and long-term priorities offering the greatest opportunities for homeland security improvement within each category. These identified issues transform into actionable strategic initiatives (see Illustration #1).

A master strategic planning worksheet for homeland security is included for the teams to download from the accompanying CD-ROM and use to list their prioritized short- and long-term initiatives. The appropriate category, term, and priority should be circled, detailing the specific initiative. Action item(s) should be listed in respective order to accomplish the identified strategies. In addition, individual responsibilities and review and completion dates should be documented to transform the organization's strategic initiatives into actionable improvement. Illustration #2 details how to complete a strategic planning worksheet for homeland security.

The strategic planning worksheet for homeland security should be completed by the assessment team (see Illustration #2). The results of both the assessment and the identified strategic issues for homeland security should be reported back to the organization's senior leadership and ultimately integrated into the organization's annual short- and long-term strategic planning process for homeland security. See homeland security plan and budget forms on the accompanying CD-ROM to develop a complete homeland security plan based on assessment findings.

ILLUSTRATION #1
1 Leadership

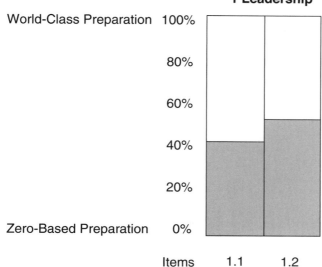

World-Class Preparation   100%

80%

60%

40%

20%

Zero-Based Preparation   0%

Items   1.1   1.2

1.1 Organizational Leadership
1.2 Social Responsibility

Note: Based on bar graphs, select and prioritize within each category short- and long-term strategic issues identified in the assessment and list below.

1 Leadership Category

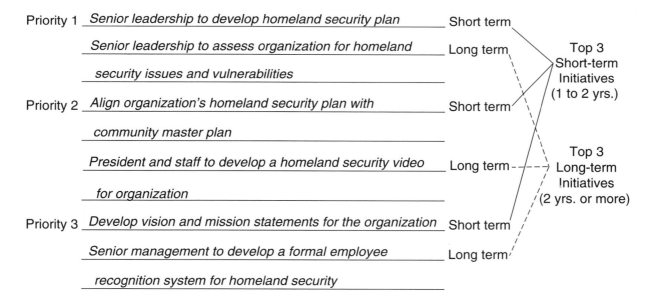

Priority 1 _Senior leadership to develop homeland security plan_   Short term

Senior leadership to assess organization for homeland   Long term

security issues and vulnerabilities

Priority 2 _Align organization's homeland security plan with_   Short term

community master plan

President and staff to develop a homeland security video   Long term

for organization

Priority 3 _Develop vision and mission statements for the organization_   Short term

Senior management to develop a formal employee   Long term

recognition system for homeland security

Top 3
Short-term
Initiatives
(1 to 2 yrs.)

Top 3
Long-term
Initiatives
(2 yrs. or more)

ILLUSTRATION #2
STRATEGIC PLANNING WORKSHEET FOR A HOMELAND SECURITY PLAN

Category (circle one)

(1 Leadership)
2 Strategic Planning
3 Customer and Market Focus
4 Measurement, Analysis, and Knowledge Management
5 Human Resource Focus
6 Process Management
7 Business Results

Term (circle one)
Short term: one to two years
Long term: more than two years

Priority (circle one)(1) 2 3   _Senior leadership to develop homeland security plan_

ACTION ITEM(S) (Steps to accomplish strategy)	WHO IS RESPONSIBLE	REVIEW DATE	COMPLETION DATE
1. _Define homeland security issues and vulnerabilities_	_President_	_January 10_	_February 28_
2. _Form a senior management team to review homeland security issues_	_Vice president_	_February 5_	_March 15_
3. _Cross-functional employee team to develop plan_	_Director_	_March 30_	_April 10_
4. _Senior staff finalizes homeland security plan_	_President and vice presidents_	_April 15_	_May 15_
5. _Distribute plan to employees, suppliers, customers, and partners_	_Managers_	_May 29_	_June 29_
6.			
7.			
8.			
9.			
10.			

| List action items in respective order | List individual responsibilities by names or position | List review dates | List completion dates |

STRATEGIC PLANNING WORKSHEET FOR A HOMELAND SECURITY PLAN

Category (circle one)

1 Leadership
2 Strategic Planning
3 Customer and Market Focus
4 Measurement, Analysis, and Knowledge Management
5 Human Resource Focus
6 Process Management
7 Business Results

Term (circle one)
Short term: one to two years
Long term: more than two years

Priority (circle one) 1   2   3 _____

ACTION ITEM(S) (Steps to accomplish strategy)	WHO IS RESPONSIBLE	REVIEW DATE	COMPLETION DATE
1. _____			
2. _____			
3. _____			
4. _____			
5. _____			
6. _____			
7. _____			
8. _____			
9. _____			
10. _____			

A Quick and Easy Supplier/Customer Assessment for Homeland Security (Based on Baldrige Criteria)

Reasons for Conducting a Homeland Security Self-Assessment for Suppliers/Customers

- To align your organization's homeland security initiatives with its suppliers/customers to save and reduce costs
- To receive a "results-oriented" supplier/customer review of homeland security readiness
- To gain knowledge of the various supplier/customer homeland security initiatives
- To identify supplier/customer strengths and opportunities for homeland security readiness
- To improve overall supplier/customer performance regarding homeland security
- To use as a tool to gauge supplier/customer progress in meeting homeland security compliance issues
- To use assessment results to help suppliers/customers develop a homeland security plan
- To encourage suppliers/customers to view homeland security readiness as a competitive issue

The Homeland Security Assessment ensures that your organization's suppliers/customers are focused on homeland security issues and aligning their homeland security goals with those of your organization.

 Forms can be downloaded from the CD-ROM located inside the back cover of this book.

171

Organizational Profile for Homeland Security

Name: _____   Date: _____

(Check one)   _____ Supplier   _____ Customer   _____ Other

Organization Environment (Describe how the organization's main products, offerings, and services are impacted by homeland security issues.)

Organizational Relationship (Describe how the organization meets homeland security needs of key customer segments, stakeholder groups, suppliers, and partners.)

Competitive Environment (Describe organization's competitive position and approach to addressing homeland security isues relative to other comparable organizations delivering similar products, offerings, and services.)

Strategic Challenges (Describe how the organization's key operations, human resources, and community-related challenges are impacted by homeland security issues.)

Performance Improvement System (Describe the organization's overall approach to performance improvement and systematic evaluation of its homeland security initiatives.)

Supplier/Customer Homeland Security Self-Assessment Evaluation Dimensions

The organization scoring system is based on three evaluation dimensions: (1) approach, (2) deployment, and (3) results. All three dimensions should be considered before assigning a score.

The Three Assessment Dimensions

Approach

Approach refers to the method(s) the organization uses to accomplish the homeland security activity. The scoring criteria used to evaluate the approach may include one or more of the following, as appropriate:

- The effectiveness of the use of methods, tools, and techniques
- The degree to which the approach embodies effective evaluation/improvement cycles
- The degree to which the approach is based upon quantitative information that is objective and reliable
- The degree to which the approach is prevention-based
- The uniqueness and innovativeness of the approach, including significant and effective new adaptations of tools and techniques used in other organizational applications
- The uniqueness of the approach

Deployment

Deployment refers to the extent to which the organization applies and/or distributes its homeland security activity among employees, customers, suppliers, stakeholders, and/or departments. The scoring criteria used to evaluate deployment may include one or more of the following, as appropriate:

- The appropriate and effective application among employees, customers, suppliers, stakeholders, and/or departments.
- The appropriate and effective application to all transactions and interactions with employees, customers, suppliers, stakeholders, and/or departments.
- The activity involves all employees.
- The activity is applied in all departments.

Results

Results refers to outcomes the organization achieves when applying the homeland security activity. The scoring criteria used to evaluate results may include one or more of the following, as appropriate:
- The rate of quality and performance improvement
- The breadth of quality and performance improvement
- The demonstration of sustained performance improvement
- The comparison with competitive and/or best practice organization initiatives
- The organization's ability to show that improvement results were derived from its strategic initiatives

Guidelines for the Supplier/Customer Homeland Security Self-Assessment

Introduction

The assessment is a carefully considered evaluation resulting in an opinion or judgment of the effectiveness and efficiency of the organization and the maturity of the organization's homeland security performance management system. Self-assessment is usually performed by the organization's own employees. The intent of the assessment is to provide fact-based guidance to the organization regarding where to invest resources for homeland security improvement.

The assessment is intended to provide an approach to determine the relative degree of maturity of the organization's homeland security performance management systems and to identify the main areas of homeland security improvement.

Specific features of the organizational self-assessment approach for homeland security are that it can:

- Be applied to the entire organizational performance management system.
- Be completed quickly with internal resources.
- Be completed by a multidiscipline team or by one person in the organization who is supported by senior leadership.
- Identify and facilitate the prioritization of the organization's strengths and opportunities for improvement.
- Facilitate maturing and aligning of the organization's homeland security initiatives and developing a homeland security plan.

Supplier/Customer Self-Assessment Scoring Profile

Approach/Deployment

Maturity Level	Performance Level	Guidance
0	Approach	No Approach
1	Approach	Good Approach/No Deployment
2	Approach	Systematic Approach/Not Fully Deployed
3	Deployment	Sound Approach/Partial Deployment
4	Deployment	Sound Approach/Mostly Deployed
5	Deployment	Sound Approach/Full Deployment

Results

Maturity Level	Performance Level	Guidance
0	Results	No Performance Results
1	Results	Some Performance Results
2	Results	Good Performance Results
3	Results	Some Trends/Good Results
4	Results	Many Improvement Trends/Good Results
5	Results	Excellent Trends/Sustained Results

Assessment Improvement Plan

List strengths and opportunities based on assessment. Align and transform key findings into a homeland security plan.

Strengths:

Opportunities:

Homeland Security Issues:

1 Leadership
(Circle one)

1. Senior leadership sets and deploys the organization's values, strategic directions, and performance expectations of homeland security initiatives.

0	1	2	3	4	5
Approach			Deployment		

2. Senior leaders create an environment for empowerment, innovation, safety, and equity for all employees regarding homeland security issues.

0	1	2	3	4	5
Approach			Deployment		

3. Organization's homeland security governance issues are addressed by senior leadership (i.e., management accountability for the organization's action, fiscal accountability, independent internal/external audits, and protection of stakeholder interests).

0	1	2	3	4	5
Approach			Deployment		

4. Senior leaders review the organization's homeland security performance and capabilities relative to competitors and comparable organizations' short- and longer-term goals and achievements.

0	1	2	3	4	5
Approach			Deployment		

5. Senior leaders identify, review, and share with stakeholders key performance measures for homeland security initiatives regularly.

0	1	2	3	4	5
Approach			Deployment		

6. Senior leaders translate key performance review findings for homeland security into priorities for organization improvements.

0	1	2	3	4	5
Approach			Deployment		

7. Organization leaders' performance regarding homeland security issues is reviewed by key stakeholders, and the findings are used to improve their leadership effectiveness.

0	1	2	3	4	5
Approach			Deployment		

8. The organization anticipates and addresses the impact that its homeland security programs, offerings, services, and operations have on the communities it serves both currently and in the future.

0	1	2	3	4	5
Approach			Deployment		

9. The organization ensures ethical behavior in all transactions and interactions involving homeland security initiatives.

0	1	2	3	4	5
Approach			Deployment		

10. The organization actively supports and strengthens homeland security initiatives within communities in which it is located.

0	1	2	3	4	5
Approach			Deployment		

✓ **Documentation**

☐ _____
☐ _____
☐ _____
☐ _____
☐ _____
☐ _____
☐ _____
☐ _____
☐ _____
☐ _____
☐ _____
☐ _____
☐ _____
☐ _____
☐ _____
☐ _____
☐ _____
☐ _____
☐ _____
☐ _____
☐ _____
☐ _____
☐ _____
☐ _____
☐ _____
☐ _____

To score, add the circled numbers together and divide by 10. Transfer score to (Supplement 1) Scheme Form.

Average Score [ ]

Note: List documents that support assessment findings.

Assessment Improvement Plan

List strengths and opportunities based on assessment. Align and transform key findings into a homeland security plan.

Strengths:

Opportunities:

Homeland Security Issues:

2 Strategic Planning
(Circle one)

1. The organization's overall homeland security strategic planning process involves all key stakeholders.

0	1	2	3	4	5
Approach			Deployment		

2. The organization's strategic planning for homeland security addresses environment, programs, offerings, technology, resources, budgetary, ethical responsibilities, supplier/customer needs, and regulatory issues.

0	1	2	3	4	5
Approach			Deployment		

3. The organization has documented its strategic objectives for homeland security and has published a timetable for accomplishing them.

0	1	2	3	4	5
Approach			Deployment		

4. The organization's strategic objectives for homeland security balance the needs of employees and key stakeholders.

0	1	2	3	4	5
Approach			Deployment		

5. The organization has developed and deployed action plans to employees to achieve its key strategic objectives for homeland security.

0	1	2	3	4	5
Approach			Deployment		

6. The organization has identified and shared with all key stakeholders its short-and longer-term action plans for homeland security.

0	1	2	3	4	5
Approach			Deployment		

7. The organization has identified human resource plans within its strategic objectives and has published action plans to ensure progress toward meeting its goals for homeland security.

0	1	2	3	4	5
Approach			Deployment		

8. The organization has identified key performance indicators for tracking action plan progress of its homeland security plan.

0	1	2	3	4	5
Approach			Deployment		

9. The organization has identified performance projections with time horizons for its strategic objectives for homeland security.

0	1	2	3	4	5
Approach			Deployment		

10. The organization has based its short and longer-term performance projections on competitors, comparable organizations, benchmarks, goals, and/or past homeland security performance.

0	1	2	3	4	5
Approach			Deployment		

✓ **Documentation**

To score, add the circled numbers together and divide by 10. Transfer score to (Supplement 1) Scheme Form.

Average Score

Note: List documents that support assessment findings.

Assessment Improvement Plan

List strengths and opportunities based on assessment. Align and transform key findings into a homeland security plan.

Strengths:

Opportunities:

Homeland Security Issues:

3 Customer and Market Focus
(Circle one)

1. The organization has a method to determine and target customer segments and markets that its homeland security program will address.

0	1	2	3	4	5
Approach			Deployment		

2. The organization has methods to listen and learn from current, former, and future customers and stakeholders regarding requirements and expectations of homeland security programs, offerings, and services.

0	1	2	3	4	5
Approach			Deployment		

3. The organization keeps its listening and learning methods current with homeland security service needs and directions (i.e., focus groups, surveys, etc.).

0	1	2	3	4	5
Approach			Deployment		

4. The organization builds relationships by providing homeland security initiatives to increase loyalty, satisfy, and retain customers.

0	1	2	3	4	5
Approach			Deployment		

5. The organization ensures that a consistent homeland security approach process is in place for employees who have direct contact with customers/stakeholders.

0	1	2	3	4	5
Approach			Deployment		

6. The organization ensures that its customer relationship skills are kept current with homeland security service needs and directions.

0	1	2	3	4	5
Approach			Deployment		

7. The organization has a method to determine customer satisfaction and dissatisfaction with homeland security initiatives.

0	1	2	3	4	5
Approach			Deployment		

8. The organization has a consistent customer follow-up procedure for its homeland security initiative programs, services, and offerings that ensures prompt and actionable feedback.

0	1	2	3	4	5
Approach			Deployment		

9. The organization compares its customer satisfaction with homeland security initiatives against competition and/or comparable organizations that deliver similar services.

0	1	2	3	4	5
Approach			Deployment		

10. The organization keeps its methods for determining customer satisfaction with homeland security initiatives current with service needs and directions (i.e., focus groups, surveys, etc.).

0	1	2	3	4	5
Approach			Deployment		

✓ **Documentation**

To score, add the circled numbers together and divide by 10. Transfer score to (Supplement 1) Scheme Form.

Average Score

Note: List documents that support assessment findings.

Assessment Improvement Plan

List strengths and opportunities based on assessment. Align and transform key findings into a homeland security plan.

Strengths:

Opportunities:

Homeland Security Issues:

4 Measurement, Analysis, and Knowledge Management
(Circle one)

1. The organization selects, collects, aligns, and integrates homeland security data and information for tracking daily operations and overall organization performance.

0	1	2	3	4	5
Approach			Deployment		

2. The organization has a selection process for homeland security to collect key comparative data and information to support operational, strategic decision making, and innovation.

0	1	2	3	4	5
Approach			Deployment		

3. The organization keeps its performance measurement system for homeland security current with organization needs and directions.

0	1	2	3	4	5
Approach			Deployment		

4. The organization collects data and information that support senior leadership's direction to accomplish the organization's homeland security strategic plans.

0	1	2	3	4	5
Approach			Deployment		

5. The organization's leadership communicates to employees homeland security data and information results that support its decision making.

0	1	2	3	4	5
Approach			Deployment		

6. The organization makes needed homeland security data and information accessible to employees, stakeholders, and suppliers/customers.

0	1	2	3	4	5
Approach			Deployment		

7. The organization ensures that homeland security hardware and software are reliable, secure, and user-friendly.

0	1	2	3	4	5
Approach			Deployment		

8. The organization keeps homeland security data and information mechanisms, including software and hardware systems, current with its needs and directions.

0	1	2	3	4	5
Approach			Deployment		

9. The organization manages the collection and transfer of homeland security knowledge among employees, stakeholders, and suppliers/customers.

0	1	2	3	4	5
Approach			Deployment		

10. The organization ensures that its data information and organizational knowledge for homeland security are timely, reliable, secure, accurate, and confidential and have integrity.

0	1	2	3	4	5
Approach			Deployment		

✓ **Documentation**

To score, add the circled numbers together and divide by 10. Transfer score to (Supplement 1) Scheme Form.

Average Score

Note: List documents that support assessment findings.

Assessment Improvement Plan

List strengths and opportunities based on assessment. Align and transform key findings into a homeland security plan.

Strengths:

Opportunities:

Homeland Security Issues:

5 Human Resource Focus
(Circle one)

✓ **Documentation**

1. The organization organizes and manages homeland security initiatives that promote cooperation, initiative, empowerment, and innovation that ensures effective communication and skill sharing among employees.

0 1 2	3 4 5
Approach	Deployment

2. The organization's homeland security performance management system supports and recognizes high-performance work among employees.

0 1 2	3 4 5
Approach	Deployment

3. The organization's homeland security initiatives identify characteristics and skills that support its recruiting, hiring, retaining, and career progression of employees.

0 1 2	3 4 5
Approach	Deployment

4. The organization's employees' education and training for homeland security contribute to achievement of action plans and directions.

0 1 2	3 4 5
Approach	Deployment

5. The organization ensures that education/training given to employees supports homeland security initiatives.

0 1 2	3 4 5
Approach	Deployment

6. The organization motivates employees to use their full potential in promoting homeland security issues and initiatives.

0 1 2	3 4 5
Approach	Deployment

7. The organization reviews and improves workplace health, safety, security, and ergonomics for homeland security.

0 1 2	3 4 5
Approach	Deployment

8. The organization ensures employee preparedness for homeland security emergencies and/or disasters.

0 1 2	3 4 5
Approach	Deployment

9. The organization has an assessment process to determine employee well-being, satisfaction, and motivation regarding homeland security issues.

0 1 2	3 4 5
Approach	Deployment

10. The organization uses assessment findings to identify and gauge employee homeland security environmental issues.

0 1 2	3 4 5
Approach	Deployment

To score, add the circled numbers together and divide by 10. Transfer score to (Supplement 1) Scheme Form.

Average Score

Note: List documents that support assessment findings.

Assessment Improvement Plan

List strengths and opportunities based on assessment. Align and transform key findings into a homeland security plan.

Strengths:

Opportunities:

Homeland Security Issues:

6 Process Management
(Circle one)

1. The organization determines value creation homeland security processes that address market needs and directions for employees and stakeholders (i.e., technology skills, problem-solving skills, team involvement, etc.).

0 1 2	3 4 5
Approach	Deployment

2. The organization determines value creation homeland security process requirements by incorporating input from employees, stakeholders, and partners.

0 1 2	3 4 5
Approach	Deployment

3. The organization incorporates new technology and organizational knowledge into the design of value creation homeland security processes.

0 1 2	3 4 5
Approach	Deployment

4. The organization has key performance measures for homeland security to control and improve its value creation processes.

0 1 2	3 4 5
Approach	Deployment

5. The organization reviews its value creation homeland security processes to maximize success and improve homeland security programs, offerings, and services.

0 1 2	3 4 5
Approach	Deployment

6. The organization determines key support processes that support its homeland security offerings (i.e., facilities management, secretarial, food service, etc.).

0 1 2	3 4 5
Approach	Deployment

7. The organization determines key support process requirements for homeland security initiatives by incorporating input from employees, stakeholders, and partners.

0 1 2	3 4 5
Approach	Deployment

8. The organization incorporates new technology and organizational knowledge into the design of support processes for homeland security.

0 1 2	3 4 5
Approach	Deployment

9. The organization has in place key performance measures to control and improve support processes of homeland security.

0 1 2	3 4 5
Approach	Deployment

10. The organization reviews its support processes to achieve better performance, to reduce variability, and to keep them current with its homeland security needs and directions.

0 1 2	3 4 5
Approach	Deployment

✓ **Documentation**

To score, add the circled numbers together and divide by 10. Transfer score to (Supplement 1) Scheme Form.

Average Score

Note: List documents that support assessment findings.

Assessment Improvement Plan

List strengths and opportunities based on assessment. Align and transform key findings into a homeland security plan.

Strengths:

Opportunities:

Homeland Security Issues:

7 Business Results
(Circle one)

1. The organization collects and trends key supplier/customer results of homeland security initiatives.

0	1	2	3	4	5
Results

2. The organization collects and trends supplier/customer and stakeholder satisfaction/dissatisfaction homeland security data and compares its results against competitive and/or comparable organizations.

0	1	2	3	4	5
Results

3. The organization collects and trends budgetary and financial performance results of homeland security initiatives.

0	1	2	3	4	5
Results

4. The organization collects and trends performance results of homeland security initiatives.

0	1	2	3	4	5
Results

5. The organization collects and trends homeland security performance and effectiveness results (i.e., employee teamwork, knowledge, and skill-sharing results, etc.).

0	1	2	3	4	5
Results

6. The organization collects and trends employee well-being, satisfaction, and dissatisfaction results for homeland security initiatives.

0	1	2	3	4	5
Results

7. The organization collects and trends operational performance of key homeland security initiatives.

0	1	2	3	4	5
Results

8. The organization collects and trends operational performance of key support service results for homeland security (i.e., productivity, cycle time, supplier/customer performance, etc.).

0	1	2	3	4	5
Results

9. The organization collects and trends data for fiscal accountability, ethical behavior, and legal compliance of homeland security issues.

0	1	2	3	4	5
Results

10. The organization collects and trends results data for its community involvement with homeland security support initiatives.

0	1	2	3	4	5
Results

✓ **Documentation**

To score, add the circled numbers together and divide by 10. Transfer score to (Supplement 1) Scheme Form.

Average Score

Note: List documents that support assessment findings.

Supplement 1—Scheme Form

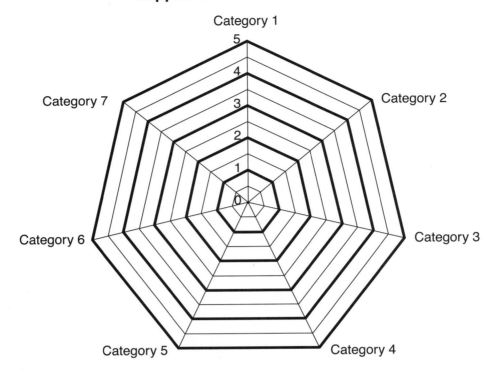

Category 1 Leadership
Category 2 Strategic Planning
Category 3 Customer and Market Focus
Category 4 Measurement, Analysis, and Knowledge Management
Category 5 Human Resource Focus
Category 6 Process Management
Category 7 Business Results

Note: Record scores from the assessment on the above radar graph.

Scoring Profile

Zero-Based Preparation   World-Class Preparation

1	2	3	4	5
Green (Low)	Blue (Guarded)	Yellow (Elevated)	Orange (High)	Red (Severe)

(Average all category scores, divide by 7, and circle appropriate number.
Refer to Homeland Security Scoring Profiles section in Chapter 1 for score descriptions.)

Risk of Attack Levels

Based on Homeland Security Advisory System (HSAS)

Organization: _____

Employees Involved: _____

Date: _____

B Homeland Security Benchmarking Process

Homeland Security Benchmarking Process

Place a check next to each step completed.

BENCHMARKING TEAM FORMATION

_____ (1) Form a homeland security benchmarking team.

_____ (2) Identify homeland security processes within the organization that need to improve.

_____ (3) List in priority order homeland security processes that offer the greatest opportunity for improvement.

_____ (4) Select a homeland security process from the prioritized list.

_____ (5) Develop a list of organizations that are known for homeland security best practices regarding the identified process.

_____ (6) Reach a consensus on a maximum of three organizations to consider for a benchmark visit (Form 2).

_____ (7) Mail out, e-mail, or fax benchmarking surveys to organizations identified by the team as exhibiting best practices (use "Benchmarking Survey," Form 1).

_____ (8) Team collects benchmarking survey data (collect data on Form 1).

_____ (9) Team reaches a consensus on survey scores.

_____ (10) Record survey scores on graphs (top half of Form 2).

_____ (11) Select benchmarking visits based on graph comparisons.

 Forms can be downloaded from the CD-ROM located inside the back cover of this book.

BENCHMARKING SITE VISIT

_____ (12) Team leader sends a formal letter requesting a site visit. (Note: Request no more than a three-hour visit.)

_____ (13) Send site visit questions with the letter requesting a site visit. (Base questions on benchmarking survey.)

_____ (14) Request in advance any information that the host organization would like to secure from the visiting organization. (All approvals must be secured from senior leadership before the site visit is made.)

_____ (15) Select two or three team members for each site visit.

_____ (16) After all site visits have been approved, secure travel and hotel accommodations for team members at each site.

_____ (17) Collect and place all pamphlets, handouts, and data received from site visit into a benchmarking folder. All findings are to be shared back on site with the entire team.

_____ (18) Team leader sends a "thank you" letter to the host organization that was benchmarked.

BENCHMARKING SITE VISIT COMPLETED

_____ (19) Review all data collected from each site visit.

_____ (20) List key findings from each site visit ("Site Visit Benchmarking Overview," Form 3).

_____ (21) Review and reach a consensus on site visit findings.

_____ (22) Incorporate findings into process improvement ("Benchmark and Process Improvement Steps," Form 4).

FORM 1: BENCHMARKING SURVEY

| _____ | _____ | _____ |
| (Name of Organization) | (Name/Title of Person Interviewed) | (Date of Phone Call/E-mail) |

This telephone or e-mail survey includes a series of questions to help the benchmark team determine which identified best practice site to visit. The highest possible score achievable by an organization is 50 points. Write the comments in the space provided; then rate the answer.

Rating Scale

Do Not Know	**World Class**	Best practice to be benchmarked_____

1 2 3 4 5   1. Do you consider your homeland security process the"best practice" within your industry? Why or why not? _____

_____

1 2 3 4 5   2. Would you rate your homeland security process against competitors' organizations as being excellent, good, or fair?_____ Why? _____

_____

1 2 3 4 5   3. How does your organization determine that your homeland security process is "best practice" within your industry? _____

_____

1 2 3 4 5   4. Does your organization collect homeland security process results? _____ Will you share your results? _____

_____

1 2 3 4 5   5. Have other organizations benchmarked your homeland security process? _____

_____

1 2 3 4 5   6. How often is your homeland security process reviewed and benchmarked against other identified best practices inside or outside your organization? _____

_____

1 2 3 4 5   7. Does your organization maintain a budget for this homeland security process? ___

_____

1 2 3 4 5   8. How many employees are involved in maintaining this homeland security process?

_____

1 2 3 4 5   9. How does this homeland security process contribute to increasing overall competitiveness for your organization? _____

_____

1 2 3 4 5   10. What impact does this homeland security process have on your overall organizational effectiveness? _____

_____

Total Points = [   ]

FORM 2: BENCHMARKING SURVEY RESULTS GRAPH

_____   _____   _____
(Organization Name)   (Organization Name)   (Organization Name)

(Questions)   **(Questions)**   **(Questions)**

World Class		1	2	3	4	5	6	7	8	9	10
	5										
	4										
	3										
Not	2										
Done	1										

Points _____   **Points** _____   **Points** _____

NOTE: Place a dot under each survey question number that best reflects the score from the survey (Form 1). Draw a line to connect the dots.

SITE VISIT SELECTIONS

(Based on benchmarking survey results)

Organization: _____   Team Leader: _____

Location: _____   Team Members: _____

Date: _____   _____

Organization: _____   Team Leader: _____

Location: _____   Team Members: _____

Date: _____   _____

Organization: _____   Team Leader: _____

Location: _____   Team Members: _____

Date: _____   _____

FORM 3: SITE VISIT BENCHMARKING OVERVIEW

Process Benchmarked: _____

Organization: Location: _____

Date: _____

Key Findings: _____

_____

_____

_____

Process Benchmarked: _____

Organization: Location: _____

Date: _____

Key Findings: _____

_____

_____

_____

Process Benchmarked: _____

Organization: Location: _____

Date: _____

Key Findings: _____

_____

_____

_____

FORM 4: BENCHMARKED PROCESS IMPROVEMENT STEPS

Process Benchmarked:_____

Proposed steps to be incorporated into an
improved process based on site visits.

	Process Steps (Present)	*Process Steps* (Based on site visits)	*Process Steps* (Improved)
1			
2			
3			
4			
5			
6			
7			
8			
9			
10			

C COUNCIL ON COMPETITIVENESS

Achieving Competitiveness and Security: Business Model

Reprinted with permission from "Achieving Competitiveness and Security: Creating a Business Case for Security" brochure
Council on Competitiveness
1500 K Street, N.W., Suite 850
Washington, D.C.

Council on Competitiveness

The Council on Competitiveness is a nonpartisan, nonprofit organization whose members are corporate chief executives, university presidents, and labor leaders dedicated to setting an action agenda to drive U.S. economic competitiveness and leadership in global markets. The council helps shape the national debate on competitiveness by concentrating on a few critical issues, including national and regional innovations, competitiveness and security, globalization, workforce development, and the benchmarking of U.S. economic performance against other countries.

The Business Case for Security (Council on Competitiveness Model)

A prospective framework for integrated security management includes the following elements:

```
                    ┌─────────────────────────┐
                    │      Leadership         │
                    │        Vision           │
                    │   Articulated Goals     │
                    └─────────────────────────┘
```

Processes	People	Plans	Tools	Partnerships
Integrated Security Management	Training Empowerment Performance	Continuity & Contingency Planning	Technology Risk Assessment Simulations	Risk-Sharing Cost-Sharing Info-Sharing

Financial Impact Assessment
Business Continuity
Market Opportunities
Productivity Gains
Competitive Advantage

- Visionary leadership and identified best practices
- Security embedded across global business processes, facilities, and supply chains
- Strategic planning for business continuity in the face of targeted attacks against companies and infrastructure
- Workforce engagement and training for embedded security
- Applied technology and risk management tools
- Public-private partnerships to share risk, cost, and information
- Assessment of financial impacts and opportunities

D Interviewing Hints and Tips

Interviewing Hints and Tips

DO'S

- Be positive when asking questions.
- Allow participants time to formulate answers.
- Make sure questions are understood.
- Reword questions to aid understanding.
- Encourage all participants to answer questions.
- Appear to be interested in all respondents' answers.
- Thank participants for their time.

DON'TS

- Do not ask questions beyond what the criteria are asking.
- Never read more into the answer than is intended by the question.
- Do not ask rhetorical questions.
- Do not disagree with answers.
- Never be repetitious when asking questions.
- Do not make loaded statements when asking questions.
- Do not allow one participant to monopolize all answers.

E Homeland Security Documentation List

(List documents that were identified in the assessment.)

Document Description	Document Date	Revision Date	Document Location	Document Owner

 Forms can be downloaded from the CD-ROM located inside the back cover of this book.

Glossary

Baldrige Assessment Terms[17]

administrative processes and support services—processes and services that may include activities and operations such as finance and accounting, software services, marketing, public relations, information services, purchasing, personnel, legal services, facilities management, research and development, secretarial, and other administrative services.

Baldrige assessment—an organizational evaluation based on the seven categories, 19 items, and 88 areas of the Malcolm Baldrige National Quality Award criteria.

benchmarking—teams of employees review and visit best practice programs, services, and practices. Benchmarking can include site visits to other organizations and telephone interviews. Benchmarking is an involved process that organizations pursue when seeking to become "world-class" in processes that they have identified as needing improvement.

business and support services—includes units and operations involving finance and accounting, software services, sales, marketing, public relations, information services, purchasing and personnel, and so forth.

business ethics—a published statement of values and business ethics that are promoted and practiced both internally and externally by the organization.

business plan—a statement of business plans and strategies that is published and shared throughout an organization. Many organizations when beginning their quality improvement process have a separate business plan and quality plan.

competitive comparisons—an organization's comparison of its products/services against major competitors and industry comparisons.

control chart—a graph that is used by employees to determine if their work process is within prescribed limits.

cross-functional teams—teams formed from different divisions or departments to solve or create new solutions to an organizational problem or opportunity.

customer—the end-user of all products and services produced within an organization. Customers are both internal and external.

customer contact employee—an employee who has direct interface with external customers, in person, via telephone, or other means.

customer relationship management—an organization's interactions and relationships with its customers.

cycle time—the amount of time it takes to complete a specified work process.

data—the collection of facts, information, or statistics.

data analysis—the breaking apart of data to help the organization gauge improvement.

documented improvement—a process improvement that has been supported against base-line data and documented at measured intervals.

ergonomics—the evaluation of an organization's facilities and equipment to ensure compatibility between workers and their work processes.

employee involvement—involvement of employees across the organization at all levels.

employee morale—the attitudes of employees in regard to their willingness to perform work tasks.

empowerment—employees' freedom to respond to customer demands and requests.

flowchart—a graphic map of a work process used by employee teams to document the current condition of a process.

goals and strategies—organizations develop goals and strategies for short-term (1 to 2 years) and long-term (2 years or more) desired results. Goals and strategies are usually written and distributed across the organization.

improvement plan—a written plan that the organization has published to accomplish desired improvement results.

internal customer/supplier network—an organization's employee network; referred to as inside customers and suppliers.

key indicators—key measures of performance (i.e., productivity, cycle time, cost, and other effectiveness measures).

manufacturing organization—an organization that makes or processes raw materials into a finished product.

measurement—the process of gauging an organization's results against its customers' requirements.

mission statement—many organizations have a published document that defines an organization's reason for existing. The mission statement is shared with employees, suppliers, and customers.

performance data—results of improvements in product and service production and delivery processes.

process—a series of steps linked together to provide a product or service for an end-user.

process control—a control device to detect and remove causes of variation to a defined process.

process management—organization's maintenance of defined processes to ensure that both quality and performance are continuously improved.

productivity improvement—measured reduction in an organization's key operational processes.

problem-solving tools—tools used by teams to solve process problems (i.e., flowcharts, Pareto analysis, histograms, control charts, cause-and-effect diagrams, and matrix diagrams).

problem-solving teams—teams of employees selected and empowered by management to assess, analyze, and solve problems within an organization. These teams may be cross-functional, work group, departmental, or project focused.

public responsibility—an organization's impact and possible impact on society with its products, services, and operations. This includes business ethics, environment, education, health care, community services, and safety as they relate to the public. Practices of trade or business associations are also considered part of an organization's public responsibility.

quality plan—a written statement of an organization's plan for maintaining and improving quality. An organization that has just begun the quality improvement process usually has this plan separate from its business plan. The more mature organizations in quality usually integrate their quality plan with their business plan.

quality results—an organization's achievement levels and improvement trends.

quality assessment—an assessment of an organization's approach to and implementation of quality.

safe work practices—an organization's promotion of safety on the worksite for employees. Many organizations have documented guidelines for employees to follow and they collect data on safe work practices.

strategic plan—a detailed plan of action developed by an organization establishing and defining measurable goals to achieve continuous quality improvement within the organization. A strategic plan can be broken into short term (1 to 2 years) and long term (more than 2 years).

survey process—the means by which an organization collects data from its customers and employees. These surveys help an organization focus on internal/external customer satisfaction issues.

senior executive—refers to the organization's highest ranking official and those reporting directly to that official.

service organization—nonmanufacturing organizations, such as utilities, schools, government, transportation, finance, real estate, restaurants, hotels, news media, business services, professional services, and repair services.

small business—complete businesses with no more than 500 full-time employees. Business activities may include manufacturing and/or service.

statistical process control (SPC)—technique for measuring and analyzing process variations.

supplier—an individual or group, either internal to the organization or external, that provides input to a work group or customer.

supplier certification program—a formal supplier program used by an organization to improve supplier quality. Many organizations partner with critical suppliers and establish a relationship of trust and measurable results.

supplier partnership—a supplier process practiced by many service and manufacturing organizations. Organizations establish a preferred supplier program that is based on a trust relationship with measurable results. Supplier partnerships are usually a prelude to a more formalized supplier certification program.

system—a set of well-defined and well-designed processes for meeting the organizations quality and performance requirements.

targets—desired goals that organizations have in their strategic planning process.

third-party survey—a survey conducted by a resource outside the organization.

total quality management (TQM)—a management philosophy that focuses on continuous quality improvement throughout an organization.

user-friendly—a process that is understandable to all levels of a workforce within an organization. A user-friendly process can be understood because it is written in simpler, more understandable language.

values statement—a published document that describes an organization's beliefs. This values statement is usually shared with faculty, staff, students, customers, suppliers, and the community.

vision statement—many organizations have a published document that defines their direction for the next 5 to 10 years. The vision statement is shared with both internal and external groups.

world-class organization—an organization that produces excellent results in major areas with a sound quality management approach to homeland security. This organization is totally integrated with a systematic prevention-based system that is continuously refined through evaluations and improvement cycles.

zero-based organization—an organization that has no quality system in place for homeland security and is anecdotal in its implementation of a sound, systematic, effective, and quality management–based approach to homeland security that is fully integrated and implemented across the organization.

Homeland Security Assessment Terms[18]

acceptable risk—the level of Residual Risk that has been determined to be a reasonable level of potential loss/disruption for a specific IT system.

access—the right to enter or use a system and its resources; to read, write, modify, or delete data; or to use software processes or network bandwidth.

access control—limiting access to information system resources to authorized users, programs, processes, or other systems only.

accountability—the explicit assignment of responsibilities for oversight of areas of control to executives, managers, staff, owners, providers, and users of minimum essential infrastructure (MEI) resource elements.

agency—federal department, major organizational unit within a department, or independent agency.

aggregated data—data that an organization has gathered together into a mass or sum so as to constitute a whole. Aggregated data is collected and used to determine an organization's achievement levels and improvement trends.

alert—notice of specific attack directed at an organization's IS resources.

application—all application systems, internal and external, used in support of the core processes.

areas of control—collectively, controls consist of the policies, procedures, practices, and organizational structures designed to provide reasonable assurance that business objectives will be achieved and that undesired events will be prevented or detected and corrected.

areas of potential compromise—these broad topical areas represent categories where losses can occur that will impact both a department or agency and its ability to conduct core missions.

assurance—grounds for confidence that a system design meets its requirements, satisfies specifications, or a specific property is satisfied.

attack—a discreet malicious action of debilitating intent inflicted by one entity upon another. An opponent might attack a critical infrastructure to destroy or incapacitate it.

audit—independent review and examination of records and activities to assess the adequacy of system controls, to ensure compliance with established security policies and procedures, and/or to recommend necessary changes in controls, policies, or procedures to meet security objectives.

audit trail—chronological records of system activities or message routing that permits the reconstruction and examination of a sequence of events.

authentication—Access privileges granted to a user, program, or process.

availability—timely, reliable access to data and information services for authorized users.

capability—the ability of a suitably organized, trained, and equipped entity to access, penetrate, or alter government or privately owned information or communications systems and/or to disrupt, deny, or destroy all or part of a critical infrastructure.

chief information officer—agency official who provides advice and other assistance to the head of the agency and other senior management personnel to ensure that information and technology is acquired and information resources are managed in a manner that implements the policies and procedures of the Congress and the priorities established by the head of the agency.

civil liberties—those individual rights and freedoms protected by the Constitution, the Bill of Rights, and federal law and regulations.

code—in computer programming, a set of symbols used to represent characters and format commands and instructions in a program. Source code refers to the set of commands and instructions making up a program.

code amber—significantly debilitate the ability of an agency to fulfill its mission, critical national security or national economic security functions, or to provide continuity of government services.

code green—no appreciable impact on agency missions.

code red—prevent an agency from fulfilling its mission, critical national security or national economic security functions, or from providing continuity of core government services. From the perspective of an attacker, this would constitute a "kill."

cold site—an alternate site with electrical and communications connections and computer equipment, but no running system; it is maintained by an organization to facilitate prompt resumption of service after a disaster.

computer emergency response team—An organization chartered by an information system owner to coordinate and/or accomplish necessary actions in response to computer emergency incidents that threaten the availability or integrity of its information systems.

computer network—a set of computers that are connected and able to exchange data.

computer security—measures and controls that ensure confidentiality, integrity, and availability of IS assets, including hardware, software, firmware, and information being processed, stored, and communicated.

confidentiality—assurance that information is not disclosed to unauthorized persons, processes, or devices.

consequence management—includes measures to protect public health and safety, restore essential government services, and provide emergency relief to governments, businesses, and individuals affected by the consequences of terrorism. The laws of the United States assign primary authority to the states to respond to the consequences of terrorism; the federal government provides assistance as required.

crisis management—includes measures to identify, acquire, and plan the use of resources needed to anticipate, prevent, and/or resolve a threat or act of terrorism.

critical infrastructures—those systems and assets—both physical and cyber—so vital to the Nation that their incapacity or destruction would have a debilitating impact on national security, national economic security, and/or national public health and safety.

cyberattack—exploitation of the software vulnerabilities of information technology–based control components.

data integrity—a condition existing when data is unchanged from its source and has not been accidentally or maliciously modified, altered, or destroyed.

debilitated—a condition of defense or economic security characterized by ineffectualness.

defense—the confidence that Americans' lives and personal safety, both at home and abroad, are protected and the United States' sovereignty, political freedom, and independence, with its values, organizations, and territory intact are maintained.

delete access—the ability to erase or remove data or programs.

denial of service—a form of attack that reduces the availability of a resource.

destruction—a condition when the ability of a critical infrastructure to provide its customers an expected upon level of products and services is negated. Typically a permanent condition. An infrastructure is considered destroyed when its level of performance is zero.

digital signature—cryptographic process used to ensure the authenticity and nonrepudiation of a message originator and/or the integrity of a message.

disaster recovery—the process of restoring an IS to full operation after an interruption in service, including equipment repair/replacement, file recovery/restoration, and resumption of service to users.

economic security—the confidence that the nation's goods and services can successfully compete in global markets while maintaining or boosting real incomes of its citizens.

emergency services—a critical infrastructure characterized by medical, police, fire, and rescue systems and personnel that are called upon when an individual or community is responding to emergencies. These services are typically provided at the local level (county or metropolitan area). In addition, state and federal response plans define emergency support functions to assist in response and recovery.

entity-wide security—planning and management that provides a framework and continuing cycle of activity for managing risk, developing security policies, assigning responsibilities, and monitoring the adequacy of the entity's physical and cyber security controls.

environment—aggregate of the external procedures, conditions, and objects affecting the development, operation, and maintenance of an IS.

event—an occurrence, not yet assessed, that may affect the performance of an IS.

execute access—the ability to execute a software program.

expert review team—security experts to assist government entities with development of internal infrastructure protection plans; the ERT is charged with improving government-wide information systems security by sharing recommended practices, ensuring consistent infrastructure frameworks, and identifying needed technical resources.

extranet—an intranet that is accessible or partially accessible to authorized users outside the organization.

facilities—all facilities required to support the core processes, including the resources to house and support information technology resources, and other resources.

firewall—an electronic boundary that prevents unauthorized users from accessing certain files on a network; or a computer used to maintain such a boundary.

firmware—application recorded in permanent or semipermanent computer memory.

gateway—interface between networks that facilitates compatibility by adapting transmission speeds, protocols, codes, or security measures.

government services—sufficient capabilities at the federal, state, and local levels of government are required to meet the needs for essential services to the public.

hacker—any unauthorized user who gains, or attempts to gain, access to an IS, regardless of motivation.

hardware—the physical components of a computer system.

hijacking—an attack that occurs during an authenticated session with a database or system. The attacker disables a user's desktop system, intercepts responses from the application, and responds in ways that prolong the session.

hot site—an alternate site with a duplicate IS already set up and running, maintained by an organization or its contractor to ensure continuity of service for critical systems in the event of a disaster.

hyperlink—an electronic link providing direct access from one distinctively marked place in a hypertext or hypermedia document to another in the same or a different document.

incapacitation—an abnormal condition when the level of products and services a critical infrastructure provides its customers is reduced. While typically a temporary condition, an infrastructure is considered incapacitated when the duration of reduced performance causes a debilitating impact.

incident—an occurrence that has been assessed as having an adverse effect on the security or performance of an IS.

information and communications—a critical infrastructure characterized by computing and telecommunications equipment, software, processes, and people that support.

information assurance—information operations that protect and defend information and information systems by ensuring their availability, integrity, authentication, confidentiality, and nonrepudiation.

information security—actions taken for the purpose of reducing system risk, specifically, reducing the probability that a threat will succeed in exploiting critical infrastructure vulnerabilities using electronic or computer-based means.

information sharing and analysis center—centers designed by the private sector that serve as a mechanism for gathering, analyzing, appropriately sanitizing, and disseminating private sector information.

information systems (IS)—the entire infrastructure, organization, personnel, and components for the collection, processing, storage transmission, display, dissemination, and disposition of information.

information technology (IT)—the hardware and software that processes information, regardless of the technology involved, whether computers, telecommunications, or other technologies.

infrastructure—the framework of interdependent networks and systems comprising identifiable industries, organizations (including people and procedures), and distribution capabilities that provide a reliable flow of products and services essential to the defense and economic security of the United States, the smooth functioning of governments at all levels, and society as a whole.

infrastructure assurance—preparatory and reactive risk management actions intended to increase confidence that a critical infrastructure's performance level will continue to meet customer expectations despite incurring threat inflicted damage. For instance, incident mitigation, incident response, and service restoration.

integrity—condition existing when an information system (IS) operates without unauthorized modification, alteration, impairment, or destruction of any of its components.

interdependence—dependence among elements or sites of different infrastructures, and therefore, effects by one infrastructure upon another.

interface—a common boundary or connector between two applications or devices, such as the graphical user interface (GUI) that allows a human user to interact with an application written in code.

internet—a decentralized, global network of computers (Internet hosts) linked by the use of common communications protocols (transmission control protocol/Internet protocol, or TCP/IP). The Internet allows users worldwide to exchange messages, data, and images.

intranet—a private network for communications and sharing of information that, unlike the Internet, is accessible only to authorized users within an organization. An organization's intranet is usually protected from external access by a firewall.

intrusion—attacks or attempted attacks from outside the security perimeter of an IS.

logic bomb—a small, malicious program that is activated by a trigger (such as a date or the number of times a file is accessed), usually to destroy data or source code.

malicious program—source code incorporated into an application that directs an IS to perform an unauthorized, often destructive, action.

metric—an agreed-upon quantitative measure of performance.

minimum level of protection—the reduction in the total risk that results from the impact of in-place safeguards.

mission critical—systems handling information that is determined to be vital to the operational readiness or mission effectiveness of deployed and contingency forces in terms of both content and timeliness and must be absolutely accurate and available on demand (may include classified information in a traditional context, as well as sensitive and unclassified information).

mitigation—preplanned and coordinated operator reactions to infrastructure warning and/or incidents designed to reduce or minimize impacts; support and complement emergency, investigatory, and crisis management response; and facilitate reconstitution.

network security—security procedures and controls that protect a network from (a) unauthorized access, modification, and information disclosure and (b) physical impairment or destruction.

operating system—software required by every computer that (a) enables it to perform basic tasks such as controlling disks, drives, and peripheral devices and (b) provides a platform on which applications can run.

optical scanner—a peripheral device that can read printed text or illustrations and translate them into a digitized image (bit map) that can be stored, displayed, and manipulated on a computer.

partnership—a relationship between two or more entities wherein each accepts responsibility to contribute a specified, but not necessarily equal, level of effort to the achievement of a common goal. The public and private sector contributing their relative strengths to protect and ensure the continued operation of critical infrastructures.

password—a string of characters containing letters, numbers, and other keyboard symbols that is used to authenticate a user's identity or authorize access to data. A password is generally known only to the authorized user who originated it.

password cracker—an application that tests for passwords that can be easily guessed, such as words in the dictionary or simple strings of characters (e.g., "abcdefgh" or "qwertyuiop").

patch—a quick modification of a program, which is sometimes a temporary fix until the problem can be solved more thoroughly.

physical security—actions taken for the purpose of restricting and limiting unauthorized access, specifically, reducing the probability that a threat will succeed in exploiting critical infrastructure vulnerabilities including protection against direct physical attacks, for example, through use of conventional or unconventional weapons.

probe—a device programmed to gather information about an IS or its users.

protocol—a set of rules and formats, semantic and syntactic, that allow one IS to exchange information with another.

public confidence—trust bestowed by citizens based on demonstrations and expectations of their government's ability to provide for their common defense and economic security and behave consistent with the interests of society; and their critical infrastructures' ability to provide products and services at expected levels and to behave consistent with their customers' best interests.

public key infrastructure—framework established to issue, maintain, and revoke public key certificates accommodating a variety of security technologies, including the use of software.

purge—to render stored applications, files, and other information on a system unrecoverable.

read access—the ability to look at and copy data or a software program.

recommended practices—generally accepted principles, procedures, and methods to ensure commonality, efficiency, and interoperability.

reconstitution—owner/operator–directed restoration of critical assets and/or infrastructure.

red team—independent and focused threat-based effort by an interdisciplinary, simulated adversary to expose and exploit vulnerabilities as a means to improve the security posture of information systems.

redundancy—duplication of system components (e.g., hard drives), information (for example, backup tapes, archived files), or personnel intended to increase the reliability of service and/or decrease the risk of information loss.

reliability—the capability of a computer, or information or telecommunications system, to perform consistently and precisely according to its specifications and design requirements, and to do so with high confidence.

remediation—deliberate precautionary measures undertaken to improve the reliability, availability, survivability, and so forth, of critical assets, and/or infrastructures, for example, emergency planning for load shedding, graceful degradation, and priority restoration; increased awareness, training, and education; changes in business practices or operating procedures, asset hardening or design improvements; and system-level changes such as physical diversity, deception, redundancy, and backups.

remote access—use of a modem and communications software to connect to a computer network from a distant location via a telephone line or wireless connection.

residual risk—the potential for the occurrence of an adverse event after adjusting for the impact of all in-place safeguards.

response—coordinated third-party (not owner/operator) emergency (e.g., medical, fire, hazardous, or explosive material handling), law enforcement, investigation, defense, or other crisis management service aimed at the source or cause of the incident.

risk—the probability that a particular critical infrastructure's vulnerability is being exploited by a particular threat weighted by the impact of that exploitation.

risk assessment—produced from the combination of threat and vulnerability assessments. Characterized by analyzing the probability of destruction or incapacitation resulting from a threat's exploitation of a critical infrastructure's vulnerabilities.

risk management—deliberate process of understanding risk and deciding upon and implementing actions to reduce risk to a defined level. Characterized by identifying, measuring, and controlling risks to a level commensurate with an assigned value.

sector—one of the two divisions of the economy (private or public).

sector coordinator—the majority of critical infrastructures are owned and operated by private sector entities.

segregation of duties—policies, procedures, and an organizational structure established so that one individual cannot control key aspects of physical and/or computer-related operations and thereby conduct unauthorized actions or gain unauthorized access to MEI resource elements.

sensitive information—unclassified information, the loss, misuse, or unauthorized disclosure or modification of which could adversely affect the national interest, the conduct of federal programs, or the privacy of individuals protected by the Privacy Act (5 U.S.C. Section 552a).

sniffer—a software or hardware tool that monitors data packets on a network to make sure messages are arriving as they should and everything else is working correctly.

software—the electronically stored commands and instructions that make an IS functional, including the operating system, applications, and communications protocols.

spoofing—unauthorized use of legitimate identification and authentication data, such as user IDs and passwords, by an intruder to impersonate an authorized user or process to gain access to an IS or data on it.

superuser—a user who is authorized to modify and control IS processes, devices, networks, and the systems.

system administrator—person responsible for the effective operation and maintenance of an IS, including implementation of standard procedures and controls to enforce an organization's security policy.

system integrity—optimal functioning of an IS, free from unauthorized impairment or manipulation.

system security officer—person assigned to implement an organization's computer security policy. Also referred to as a system security program manager.

system security plan—a formal document listing the tasks necessary to meet system security requirements, a schedule for their accomplishments, and to whom responsibilities for each task are assigned.

technology—broadly defined, includes processes, systems, models and simulations, hardware, and software.

threat—a foreign or domestic entity possessing both the capability to exploit a critical infrastructure's vulnerabilities and the malicious intent of debilitating defense of economic security. A threat may be an individual, an organization, or a nation.

time bomb—a type of logic bomb that is triggered by the arrival of a date or time.

transportation—a critical infrastructure characterized by the physical distribution system critical to supporting the national security and economic well-being of this nation, including the national airspace system, airlines and aircraft and airports; roads and highways, trucking and personal vehicles; ports and waterways and the vessels operating thereon; mass transit, both rail and bus; pipelines, including natural gas, petroleum, and other hazardous materials; freight and long-haul passenger rail; and delivery services.

Trojan horse—program containing hidden code allowing the unauthorized collection, falsification, or destruction of information.

utility—a program that performs a specific task for an IS, such as managing a disk drive or printer.

virus—a small, self-replicating, malicious program that attaches itself to an executable file or vulnerable application and delivers a payload that ranges from annoying to extremely destructive. A file virus executes when an infected file is accessed. For example, a macro virus infects the executable code embedded in Microsoft Office programs that allows users to generate macros.

vulnerability—a characteristic of a critical infrastructure's design, implementation, or operation that renders it susceptible to destruction or incapacitation by a threat.

vulnerability assessment—an examination of the ability of a system or application, including current security procedures and controls, to withstand assault. A vulnerability assessment may be used to (a) identify weaknesses that could be exploited and (b) predict the effectiveness of additional security measures in protecting information resources from attack.

Reference List for Added Reading

Anderson, R. J. (2001). *Security engineering: A guide to building dependable distributed systems.* New York: John Wiley & Sons.

Badey, T. (2003). *Annual editions: Homeland security 04/05.* New York: McGraw-Hill/Duskin.

Bosworth, S., & Kobay, M. E. (2002). *Computer security handbook.* New York: John Wiley & Sons.

Erbschloe, M. (2003). *Implementing homeland security for enterprise IT.* New York: Digital Press.

Haddow, G., & Bullock, J. (2003). *Introduction to emergency management.* New York: Butterworth-Heinemann.

Hoffman, B. (1999). *Inside terrorism.* New York: Columbia University Press.

Hutton, D. B., & Mydlanz, A. (2003). *Guide to homeland security.* New York: Barron's Educational Series.

O'Hanlon, M. E., Orszag, P. R., Liton, R. E., & Destler, I. M. (2002). *Achieving homeland security.* Portland, OR: Brookings Institution Press.

Ranum, M. J. (2003). *The myth of homeland security.* New York: John Wiley & Sons.

Ratner, M. A., & Ratner, D. (2003). *Nanotechnology and homeland security: New weapons for new wars.* New York: Prentice Hall PTR.

How to order or download current copies of the Baldrige Criteria for Performance Excellence

Criteria for Performance Excellence
Baldrige National Quality Program
National Institute of Standards and Technology
Administration Building, Room A600
100 Bureau Drive, Stop 1020
Gaithersburg, MD 20899-1020
E-mail: nqp@nist.gov
Web address: http://www.quality.nist.gov

Notes

1. *Securing the Homeland, Strengthening the Nation* by President George W. Bush, January 2002.
2. *Homeland Security: Practical Tools for Local Governments* by National League of Cities, November 2002.
3. *Preparing for Terrorism: What Every Manager Needs to Know* by Howard Levitin, MD, FACEP, International City/County Management Association (ICMA), 2001.
4. *The National Strategy for Homeland Security*, Office of Homeland Security, July 2002.
5. *The National Strategy for Homeland Security*, Office of Homeland Security, July 2002.
6. NIST, *Baldrige National Quality Program Criteria for Performance Excellence*. Gaithersburg, MD: National Institute of Standards and Technology.
7. NIST, *Baldrige National Quality Program Criteria for Performance Excellence*. Gaithersburg, MD: National Institute of Standards and Technology.
8. NIST, 2004 *Baldrige National Quality Program Criteria for Performance Excellence*. Gaithersburg, MD: National Institute of Standards and Technology.
9. *Homeland Security Presidential Directive—3*, President George W. Bush, March 2002.
10. Leadership Category 1 has been rewritten and revised for an organizational assessment of homeland security and simplified based on the Baldrige National Quality Program Criteria for Performance Excellence.
11. Strategic Planning Category 2 has been rewritten and revised for an organizational assessment of homeland security and simplified based on the Baldrige National Quality Program Criteria for Performance Excellence.
12. Customer and Market Focus Category 3 has been rewritten and revised for an organizational assessment of homeland security and simplified based on the Baldrige National Quality Program Criteria for Performance Excellence.
13. Measurement, Analysis, and Knowledge Management Category 4 has been rewritten and revised for an organizational assessment of homeland security and simplified based on the Baldrige National Quality program criteria for performance excellence.
14. Human Resource Focus Category 5 has been rewritten and revised for an organizational assessment of homeland security and simplified based on the Baldrige National Quality Program Criteria for Performance Excellence.
15. Process Management Category 6 has been rewritten and revised for an organizational assessment of homeland security and simplified based on the Baldrige National Quality Program Criteria for Performance Excellence.
16. Business Results Category 7 has been rewritten and revised for an organizational assessment of homeland security and simplified based on the Baldrige National Quality Program Criteria for Performance Excellence.
17. NIST, *Baldrige National Quality Award Program Criteria for Performance Excellence*. Gaithersburg, MD: National Institute of Standards and Technology .
18. Critical Infrastructure Assurance Office (CIAO) Report to the President of the United States on the status of Federal Critical Infrastructure Protection Activities (discontinued website) www.ciao.gov/ciao_document_library/glossary/a.htm

About the Author

Donald C. Fisher, Ph.D.

Donald Fisher, executive director of Mid-South Quality/Productivity Center—The Quality Center (a partnership between the Memphis Regional Chamber and Southwest Tennessee Community College) in Memphis, Tennessee, a Tennessee Board of Regents Center of Quality Emphasis, has presented the Malcolm Baldrige Award Criteria internationally to Hitachi, Ltd. in Japan, to the Center for Productivity in Maracaibo, Venezuela, and to a group of international suppliers in London. He has also consulted with officials from the Venezuelan Ministry of Development who have reviewed adopting the Malcolm Baldrige Criteria as a model for their National Quality Award. He has worked as a visiting scholar (commissioned by the World Bank) with the president and prime minister of Mauritius to oversee that nation's first-ever Baldrige award program. In addition, he worked with Federal Express in Dubai, United Arab Emirates, on its Baldrige Application for the Dubai Quality Award. He has worked with 85 presidents of worldwide companies owned by the Hong Leong management group in Kuala Lumpur, Malaysia, to help them use Baldrige Criteria for strategic planning. Fisher also serves as an advisor for the Gate Gourmet International (a division of SwissAir) "Global Service Excellence" Baldrige project in Zurich, Switzerland.

Fisher is a multiyear veteran of the Board of Examiners for the prestigious Malcolm Baldrige National Quality Award, and has judged quality performance based on the Baldrige Criteria for more than 100 leading organizations worldwide. He has traveled the world helping organizations with awards similar to the Baldrige Award.

He is the author or coauthor of a number of books, including *The Simplified Baldrige Award Organization Assessment, Demystifying Baldrige, Measuring Up to the Baldrige, Baldrige on Campus,* and *The Baldrige Workbook for Healthcare.* In addition, he serves on numerous quality boards throughout the United States and the world.

He presently serves as a judge for the Arizona State Quality Award, and was a founding member of the board of directors and one of six judges for the Tennessee Quality Award. He is also a past member of the advisory board and the panel of judges for the Commonwealth of Kentucky Quality Award, and has served as both a director and judge for the Greater Memphis Award for Quality. In addition to these appointments, he served on both the President's Quality Award Program panel of judges in Washington, DC, and was selected as one of eight senior judges for the Secretary of the Air Force Unit Quality Award. He served as a consultant to the National Association of College and University Business Officers (NACUBO) national project on developing its Baldrige-Based Management Achievement Award (MAA) for American colleges and universities. In addition, he served seven years as a judge for the RIT/USA Today Quality Cup Team Award.

Fisher's credentials for writing this book include spending over five years researching homeland security issues at the Federal Bureau of Investigation in Washington, related to the

McCarthy era of the 1950s. He wrote his doctoral dissertation on J. Edgar Hoover's investigation of atomic scientists during the McCarthy era, and collected more than 1000 "confidential" documents through the Freedom of Information Act. Fisher received his Ph.D. from the University of Mississippi.

His extensive research, along with his early involvement as a Baldrige examiner, gives Fisher unique knowledge and credentials related to homeland security and the use of the Baldrige Criteria as a homeland security assessment tool.

Fisher has developed a homeland security training system called Process Activated Training System® (PATS), which is used by the U.S. Postal Service. This system has been used to transform best practice security initiatives into training scripts. Contact Dr. Fisher at http://www.msqpc.com.

Index

mitigation, 208
motivation and career development, 102, 109, 110, 113

N

National Governor's Association, 1
National Guard, 11
National League of Cities, 2
national security information, 84
"National Strategy for Homeland Security Report" (2002), 2
network security, 208
New Cities Foundation, 1
newsletters, 107

O

Office of Homeland Security, 1
on-the-job training (OJT), 104, 106–108
online knowledge management system, 90
operating system, 209
operational performance, 149–150
optical scanner, 209
orange level, 10–11
organization assessment, 20–22
organization and management of work, 94–97
organizational assessment bar graph, 162–166
organizational culture, 94, 96
organizational effectiveness results, 148–151
world-class organization, 148–151
zero-based organization, 148–151
organizational governance, 34
audits, 34, 37
fiscal accountability, 34, 37
management accountability, 34, 37
stakeholder/shareholder interests, 34, 37
organizational knowledge, 86, 90–91.
See also measurement, analysis, and knowledge management
accuracy, 86, 91
best practices for, 86
confidentiality, 86, 91
customers, suppliers, partners, 86, 90
employee knowledge, 86, 90
integrity, 86, 91
reliability, 86, 91
security, 86, 91
timeliness, 86, 91
organizational leadership, 34–41
organizational governance, 34, 37

organizational performance review, 34, 38–41
senior leadership direction, 34–36
world-class organization, 35–41
zero-based organization, 35–41
organizational learning and listening, 3, 64, 67
organizational overview, 11, 23–28
organizational performance
data and information, 80–81
measurement and analysis of, 80–85
performance analysis, 84–85
performance measurement, 80–83
organizational performance review, 34
continuous/breakthrough improvement, 34, 40
key performance measures, 34, 39
readiness and capabilities, 34, 38
senior leaders review, 34, 41
organizational strategy, 148, 151

P

partners, 128–129, 148
partnership, 209
password, 209
password cracker, 209
patch, 209
peer coaching teams, 96
performance analysis, 80
communicating results, 85
organizational performance, 84–85
senior leaders' organizational performance review, 84
strategic plan, 84
performance data, 204
performance levels (Le), 6, 9, 18
performance measurement
action plan, 55, 59–60
annual review for, 83
best practices comparisons, 82
comparative data and information, 82
data selection, collection, and integration, 81
homeland security advisory system and, 81
keeping system current, 83
organizational performance, 80–83
risk of attack levels, 82
performance projection, 55, 60
personal learning, 3
physical security, 209
pilot tests, 126
pre-assessment meeting, 21
preparedness
anchor point, 7
first steps for, 2

homeland security scoring profiles, 12–18
readiness and capabilities, 38
strategic objectives for, 53, 55
in workplace, 110, 112
world-class preparation, 7
zero-based preparation, 7
probe, 209
problem-solving teams, 204
problem-solving tools, 204
process, 204
defined, 5
process control, 204
process evaluation dimension (Baldrige categories 1-6), 5–6, 8, 12–17
approach, deployment, learning, and integration (A-D-L-I), 5, 12–17
customer and market focus, 62–76
human resource focus, 93–116
leadership, 33–46
measurement, analysis, and knowledge management, 79–92
process management, 119–134
strategic planning, 49–60
process management, 3, 17, 31, 119, 204
assessment team, 21
organizational assessment bar graph, 164
supplier/customer assessment, 199
support processes, 132–138
value creation processes, 120–126
world-class organization, 120–134
zero-based organization, 120–134
product and service results, 139–140
product/service delivery, 138, 141
world-class organization, 141
zero-based organization, 141
productivity, 5, 110, 120, 148
productivity improvement, 204
profitability, 120
protocol, 209
public confidence, 209
public events, 1, 11
public key infrastructure, 209
public-private partnerships, 198
public responsibility, 42–44, 192
purge, 209

Q

quality assessment, 204
quality plan, 204
quality results, 204